JENNIFER ANISTON

JENNIFER ANISTON

The unofficial and unauthorised biography of
JENNIFER ANISTON
by Andrew Adamides

Published by
Kandour Ltd
1-3 Colebrook Place
London N1 8HZ

This edition printed in 2004 for
Bookmart Limited
Registered Number 2372865
Trading as Bookmart Ltd
Blaby Road
Wigston
Leicester LE18 4SE

First published June 2004

ISBN 1–904756–10–7

Production services:
Metro Media Ltd

Author: Andrew Adamides

With thanks to: Jenny Ross, Emma Hayley,
Lee Coventry, Belinda Weber

Cover design: Mike Lomax
Cover Image: Rex Features

Inside Images: Rex Features

© Kandour Ltd

Printed and bound by Nørhaven Paperback, Denmark

JENNIFER ANISTON

FOREWORD

This series of biographies is a celebration of celebrity. It features some of the world's greatest modern-day icons including movie stars, soap personalities, pop idols, comedians and sporting heroes. Each biography examines their struggles, their family background, their rise to stardom and in some cases their struggle to stay there. The books aim to shed some light on what makes a star. Why do some people succeed when others fail?

Written in a light-hearted and lively way, and coupled with the most up-to-date details on the world's favourite heroes and heroines, this series is an entertaining read for anyone interested in the world of celebrity. Discover all about their career highlights – what was the defining moment to propel them into superstardom? No story about fame is without its ups and downs. We reveal the emotional rollercoaster ride that many of these stars have been on to stay at the top. Read all about your most adored personalities in these riveting books.

JENNIFER ANISTON

CONTENTS

JENNIFER ANISTON

FACT FILE

Full name: Jennifer Linn Aniston
Eye colour: Brown
Hair colour: Brown
Date of birth: 11 February 1969
Place of birth: Sherman Oaks, California, USA
Height: 5' 6"
Parents: Father is John Aniston, actor/soap star. Mother is Nancy, actress and model.
Marriages: Brad Pitt, actor, on July 29, 2000 in Malibu, California. Previously had long-term relationship with actor Tate Donovan.
Children: None yet, but watch this space!

Star sign: Aquarius
Aquarius is the 11th sign in the Zodiac, and those born under this sign are noted humanitarians, philanthropists and try their very best to make the world a better place. They are progressives and visionaries who have many treasured friends. Aquarius is symbolised by the water-bearer, and Aquarians love to give the world their thoughts and ideas. They are capable of coming up with some incredibly wonderful things and like it when everyone else agrees with their ideas! They can be impatient and temperamental and can also be a bit eccentric, but usually are so lovable that their

FACT FILE

eccentricities are overlooked.

Jennifer's horoscope shows that she was born with her sun in Aquaries, making her independent, artistic and highly intelligent. Her actions can range from shy and retiring to out-and-out rebellious. Her sun is Square Mars, which gives her impulsiveness and something of a quick temper too! Her sun is also Square Neptune, which can cause a slight lack of self-esteem and make her happier in a fantasy world than in reality.

Jennifer's moon is in Sagittarius, making her a free spirit who doesn't like to be tied down. Full of optimism and idealism, Jennifer's life won't exactly be the most streamlined and she'll prefer her home life to be rather less than conventional in its organisation.

With her Mercury in Aquarius, Jennifer will always go for the most advanced concepts and should be streets ahead of everyone else in embracing them. She also has a liking for philosophy, and is broad-minded, with a good sense of judgement. In addition, she's very resourceful – and not easily swayed from going after what she wants.

Her Venus is in Aries, which means she also goes after what she wants in affairs of the heart. Passionate and impulsive about partners, she also

FACT FILE

goes for physical attractiveness and will be an exciting partner to have around. With her Venus opposite Jupiter in Libra, she likes to flash her cash (hence the wedding), spending freely.

Her Mars is in Scorpio, further enforcing her determination. She's a strong woman who won't be defeated. This also means she should have a pretty high sex-drive!

Other famous Aquarians include: Emma Bunton, Geena Davis, Tatyana Ali, Eartha Kitt, Ellen DeGeneres, Paul Newman, Nick Carter, Joey Fatone, Ed Burns, Heather Graham, Oprah Winfrey, Tom Selleck, Gene Hackman, Phil Collins, Vanessa Redgrave, Justin Timberlake, Boris Yeltsin, Lisa Marie Presley, Christie Brinkley, Farrah Fawcett, Chris Rock, Nick Nolte, Seth Green, Mia Farrow, Laura Dern, Burt Reynolds, Christina Ricci, Jane Seymour, John McEnroe, Michael Jordan, Rene Russo, Cybill Shepherd, John Travolta, Matt Dillon.

JENNIFER ANISTON

Chinese birth sign: Monkey

Jennifer's Chinese sign is the ruler of the hours 3pm to 5pm, its direction is West/Southwest, it's season Summer and month August, it's element is Metal positive and of the Yin/Yang elements, it is Yang.

Monkeys are, as a rule, excellent at becoming masters of whatever they decide to turn their hand to, and are also very successful in general. They possess the perfect combination of personality traits for this, being charming, intelligent, quick-witted and flexible. They are determined and relish nothing more than a good challenge! They won't give up easily and can be sneaky and enjoy competition, but can be a little self-centred and narcissistic. They also almost always believe themselves to be superior to all others around them!

Their self-belief is absolutely solid – they always have a good reason as to why they've done something and although they have a tendency to be impartial, are very intellectually high-powered and have very good memories. Monkeys are also very, very inquisitive!

In the year of the Monkey, absolutely anything, no matter how bizarre or unlikely, is possible. Everyone's cup will run over with

FACT FILE

success! It's a fabulous year where everyone's so drunk on happiness and success they'll barely know what's happening.

Being born on 11 February 1969 makes Jennifer an Earth Monkey, which makes her additionally motivated by her curiosity, good natured, methodical and very dependable.

JENNIFER ANISTON

At 11-years-old, she had one of her paintings displayed as part of an exhibition at the New York Metropolitan Museum of Art, alongside priceless pictures painted by some of the world's greatest.

Aniston topped the 2003 Forbes Top 100 Celebrity list, deposing the 2002 winner Britney Spears by earning $35 million in 2002 and appearing on more magazine covers than any rival celebrity.

1

Introduction

JENNIFER ANISTON

INTRODUCTION

S he's been a 'Friend' to countless millions worldwide, and overcame numerous hurdles to rise to the very top of her field. From a shy girl with a dream of being a famous actress, through being reduced to painting scenery for high school plays, appearing in a series of flop TV shows and one rather bad movie, Jennifer Aniston has persevered, finally finding success at the very top of the TV tree.

Bringing the same determination that got her a part on the world's best-loved TV series to her attempts at a film career, she's also worked her way from rom-com cutie up to serious,

JENNIFER ANISTON

INTRODUCTION

respected actress and box office draw, intelligently combining indie, cult and comedy movies into a blossoming career which looks set to shoot her to the heights of Hollywood's A-list. She's also found love with one of the world's most desirable men and this is her story...

2

The one where
it all began

JENNIFER ANISTON

THE ONE WHERE IT ALL BEGAN

Jennifer Aniston's life began on 11 February 1969, in the comfortable middle-class Sherman Oaks suburb of Los Angeles.

Given her future, if it wasn't fitting enough that she was born in the movie capital of the world, both her parents were also in show business. In fact it almost seems fated that she was to follow in their footsteps. Her father John had been brought to America from his native Crete by his parents when he was just 10 and the family moved to Pennsylvania, shortened their name from Anastassakis to the easier-to-pronounce Aniston, and opened a restaurant. Like so many others, he

THE ONE WHERE IT ALL BEGAN

dreamed of fame and fortune and had made the trek to Hollywood where he'd become an actor, and had met and married actress and model Nancy Dow, in 1965.

While he would never know the global superstardom his daughter would achieve, John did well enough as a jobbing actor, snagging plenty of guest parts on now-classic Sixties US TV shows like *Combat!*, *I Spy*, *87th Precinct*, *The Virginian* and *Mission: Impossible*. Just as Jennifer would 20 years later, he also did plenty of stage work, appearing in musicals like *Little Mary Sunshine* on Broadway, and in *Death of a Salesman* in LA.

Originally from New York, Nancy moved to LA with her family in her teens, and with her stunning looks, gravitated to the showbiz world. She too appeared in TV guest parts on series like *The Wild Wild West* and *The Beverly Hillbillies*, as well as getting behind-the-scenes work at Universal Studios, where, among other things, she 'prepared' pictures of movie-star Rock Hudson. After making just one movie appearance, in a little-seen 1969 B-movie slasher horror called *The Ice House*, Nancy all but quit acting and gave birth to Jennifer one year later.

Jennifer's earliest years in Hollywood were

THE ONE WHERE IT ALL BEGAN

pretty secure in the home she shared with her parents, and older half-brother John. Two years before she was born, her father had been cast in a regular role on the popular long-running soap *Days of Our Lives*. But this comfortable state of affairs would unfortunately not last for long. In 1970, John's character was written out of the show, and with his departure went the family's security. Typecast, John found himself having to work as a door-to-door salesman, unable to score any acting work except for two guest appearances on hit detective drama *Kojak*, alongside family friend Telly Savalas, who was also Jennifer's godfather. Times were tough, and even though Nancy secured a few modelling contracts which brought in some cash, the Aniston family found themselves with little money to go round.

Considering a career change, John wondered about becoming a doctor, but this new plan seemed doomed as well, as he was turned down by all the American universities he applied to. It seemed that he was too old for medical studies in the US. There was, however, an alternative: he could take the family back to Greece and study there.

And so at just five-years-old, and the family relocated to the Greek capital Athens, so that her

THE ONE WHERE IT ALL BEGAN

father could begin medical training there in the hope of a better life for them all.

However turbulent this must have been for little Jennifer, a long stay in Greece wasn't on the cards for the Anistons either. After the family had spent just one year in Athens, John's New York agent called with the offer of a part on another soap opera, *Love of Life*, which was filmed in New York. John accepted the part, and the family uprooted all over again, moving back to the US, and this time settling in the Big Apple.

By one of those strange showbiz quirks of fate, John's son on *Love of Life* was played by future *Superman*, Christopher Reeve. When Jennifer was nine, she and her mother bumped into Reeves on the street, but Jennifer was too embarrassed to talk to him. Just days later *Superman* opened, and Jennifer was kicking herself for not letting her mother persuade her to have a chat with the guy who was now the biggest star in town.

While it may have seemed that *Love of Life* provided Jennifer with some sort of family stability, this wasn't going to be the case. The constant upheavals had taken their toll on John and Nancy's marriage, which crumbled under the pressure. In 1978, when Jennifer was nine, John and Nancy

THE ONE WHERE IT ALL BEGAN

divorced. Ironically, after the divorce, John found his greatest TV successes, appearing for seven years on another soap, *Search for Tomorrow*, and then returning to *Days of Our Lives* in 1985 as another character, Viktor Kyriakis, a role he has reprised on and off to this day. John has also recently appeared in US smash-hits like *Star Trek: Voyager* and *The West Wing*. He got remarried to actress Sherry Rooney.

The divorce was hard on nine-year-old Jennifer. For the first year after her parents split, she didn't see her father at all, living with her mother on the 21st floor of an apartment building in a not particularly good area of New York. Eventually, though, she began spending weekends with John at his place in nearby New Jersey, and like so many children hit by divorce, Jennifer was determined to try and get her parents back together, at first trying her hardest to please them both. But it didn't work.

Having been sent to New York's well-respected Rudolf Steiner School, Jennifer then tried another familiar tactic and started behaving as badly as possible, in the hope that on the many occasions that John and Nancy were both called in to see the headmaster about her, the two would regain their spark and get back together. Needless to say, that didn't work either – although Jennifer was by this time displaying one of the personality characteristics which would do well for her in the future: a very steely determination to get what she wanted, even if in this case, it didn't work. She kept trying.

Not only was her schoolwork affected by the constant upheavals at home, but the highly imaginative little girl also found the school's strict rules oppressive. And the rules were pretty harsh, spilling over into the pupils' home lives. TV was all but forbidden, and Jennifer only got to watch it on the rare occasions when her big brother John would babysit for her. Describing her as "the queen of make-believe", John would later tell interviewers how Jennifer had a passion for TV and would copy the scenes playing out on-screen with her dolls.

While she didn't exactly respond to the school's strict regime, Jennifer did join the drama club, which she enjoyed hugely, and also developed a massive passion for art – painting and drawing to her heart's content. At 11, she even had one of her paintings displayed as part of an exhibition at the New York Metropolitan Museum of Art, alongside priceless pictures painted by some of the

THE ONE WHERE IT ALL BEGAN

world's greatest.

With her background and fascination for all things creative, it seemed almost certain that Jennifer would go into some sort of creative profession. Art, perhaps, or music – at 12, she was a huge Duran Duran fan, even camping out all night outside the band's hotel in the hope of seeing star Simon Le Bon in the flesh. Years later, in an interview given while she was promoting the movie *Rock Star*, Jennifer laughed that "I was a Duran Duran freak – and freak is the perfect word to describe my behaviour during that decade!"

Two years later, she was going out with a punk rocker from the ultra-bohemian East Village, had cut her hair into an almost-mohawk and adorned herself with as many earrings and bracelets as she possibly could. But as far as a career went, she'd already made her choice – like so many little girls in the Seventies, Jennifer was fascinated by the hit TV show *Fame*, set at New York's High School for the Performing Arts, and had decided that she was going to be an actress. She was certainly more set on that decision than she was about being a punk, admitting later that she never even really enjoyed listening to the likes of the Sex Pistols, and would have been happier

THE ONE WHERE IT ALL BEGAN

with Van Morrison or Aerosmith, but that all her rebellion was yet another act that she hoped would reunite her parents. Obviously, she was still determined on that score...

While Jennifer would one day be considered one of the most beautiful women in the world, with her posters adorning the walls of millions of teenage boys and plenty of cosmetics contracts to prove it, as a young girl she wasn't confident about the way she looked. She suffered from a weak muscle in her right eye, which made her slightly cross-eyed, and gave her poor coordination. As a result she was bad at sports and got tired very quickly when trying to read, skipping paragraphs by accident and having to go back and re-read them.

Leaving Rudolf Steiner, Jennifer auditioned for the High School for the Performing Arts and was accepted, her determination and natural talent taking her one step closer to her goal. But she was going to need every ounce of that famous determination, because she was still battling insecurities about her looks, and a resulting lack of confidence.

Jennifer's relationship with her mother compounded her self-doubt. Having spent so long as a model and actress, Nancy would talk endlessly

THE ONE WHERE IT ALL BEGAN

about people's physical appearance and make-up, which unfortunately made her daughter feel far worse about herself than she already did. In interviews later, Jennifer would say of her mother that "I don't know if I would have known how beautiful she was if she wasn't always pointing out how un-beautiful I was".

But in spite of the challenges life seemed to keep throwing at her, Jennifer forged ahead, gritting her teeth when she was passed over for the lead parts in school productions, making the best she could out of smaller character roles, and helping out behind the scenes, working on the lighting or helping to build sets. Far from the glamourous leading-lady life she'd one day lead...

And she still had the steely determination to succeed which drove her on in spite of all the apparent obstacles in her way. Any opportunity which did arrive she would take full advantage of. In an interview, her father John once remembered an instance when he invited his 15-year-old daughter to visit him on the *Days of Our Lives* set. Leaving her alone briefly in his dressing room, he came back to find her on the phone to his agent, discussing the possibility of his sending her up for movie parts.

JENNIFER ANISTON

THE ONE WHERE IT ALL BEGAN

As time went on, Jennifer's confidence in herself as a performer grew and grew, and she found something else she was good at: comedy. Through her performances, she became more and more adept at making audiences laugh. Still thinking of herself as lacking-in-the-looks-department would prove to be an enormous blessing in disguise, as Jennifer started to rely on being funny to make sure she was noticed and remembered. Teachers and students alike took notice, with the school's professors encouraging her comic skills, as well as her dramatic talent, making sure she didn't rely just on being the funny girl instead of getting deeper under a character's skin. Those who studied alongside her also remember her: by graduation she already had an agent representing her for TV adverts, and she wowed the crowds at the school's graduation performances.

Finally out of high school, Jennifer considered moving on to college like so many of her peers, but then decided against it, preferring to throw herself body and soul into acting instead.

Which she did, her life yet again parallelling events on the sitcom which would eventually make her world-famous, as like *Friends'* Rachel, she moved into a shared apartment and supported

THE ONE WHERE IT ALL BEGAN

herself by waitressing (although with rather more success than on-screen!) while also hitting the audition circuit for the New York theatre.

Her talent and drive won her parts in off-Broadway plays like *For Dear Life* at the New York Public Theater and *Dancing On Checker's Grave*. But Jennifer swiftly tired of the New York scene and was advised to try her luck on the West Coast. Jennifer took a deep breath, packed her bags, bade farewell to New York City, and headed for Los Angeles to move in with her father.

3

The one with
all the struggle

JENNIFER ANISTON

THE ONE WITH ALL THE STRUGGLE

O n her arrival in LA, the 20-year-old Jennifer certainly wasn't an overnight sensation, but she didn't starve either, winning small roles in TV movies and series. Trouble was that while these paid the rent, they weren't exactly career-boosters. In fact most were exactly the opposite.

First up was a 1990 TV movie entitled *Camp Cucamonga*, in which Jennifer appeared. Set, unsurprisingly, at a summer camp for teenagers, the film's "wacky" plotline revolved around the camp's owner believing that a local handyman is, in fact, a camp inspector, there to review the place and possibly shut it down. Jennifer played his

THE ONE WITH ALL THE STRUGGLE

daughter, who rejoiced in the incredibly awful name of Ava Schector. Attempting to cash in by casting several more-or-less teenage US sitcom stars, the film threw the unknown Jennifer into a mix which included Candace Cameron from *Full House*, Danica McKellar and Josh Saviano from *The Wonder Years*, Jaleel White from *Family Matters* and, er, Lauren Tewes from the original *Love Boat*. Also on hand was a pre-*Dr Quinn Medicine Woman* Chad Allen, a young Breckin Meyer and, amazingly enough, *Cheers'* John Ratzenberger as Jennifer's father. However, none of them could prevent the movie from being a disaster.

Next came a part on a sitcom entitled *Molloy*, where Jennifer played second fiddle to actress Mayim Bialik, better known as *Blossom*. But *Molloy* was cancelled before it completed a full season.

In between her low-key TV appearances, Jennifer made ends meet by waitressing, selling timeshare apartments, being a messenger and answering phones as a production company receptionist, juggling whatever job she had that week with the usual round of auditions. Ever independent, she also moved out of her father's place, moving to the trendy Laurel Canyon area, known as The Hill.

JENNIFER ANISTON

THE ONE WITH ALL THE STRUGGLE

At The Hill, Jennifer found some kindred spirits to make her Hollywood days seem less depressing, as she hung out with a group of young wannabe writers, actors, directors and production executives. Each Sunday, the group would cheer each other up by holding a barbecue, and, like a certain fictional group of friends would later on, they did all sorts of other zany things together, like celebrating Jennifer's 22nd birthday by sticking photos of an actor she had a crush on all over her apartment, or going on road-trips, including one in which eight of them stayed in one hotel room in Santa Barbara for three days.

With the Hill crew, Jennifer found support. As she would later tell *Rolling Stone* magazine's Rich Cohen, "everybody watched out for everybody".

Other acting work came along for Jennifer as well. She was cast in what looked like a plum part in the TV sitcom version of the smash hit film *Ferris Bueller's Day Off*, in which Charlie Schlatter took over from Matthew Broderick as the high school student who could wrap parents, teachers and peers round his little finger and couldn't put a foot wrong. Jennifer was to play Ferris' hapless sister Jeannie. In another twist, Jennifer Grey, the actress who played Jeannie in

THE ONE WITH ALL THE STRUGGLE

the film, appeared in *Friends* as Mindy, Rachel's maid of honour, who eventually married Barry the orthodontist who Rachel ditched at the altar.

In the event, the *Ferris Bueller* series failed miserably and lasted just 13 episodes before it joined *Molloy* on the TV scrapheap, putting Jennifer out of work again. But life at The Hills was still fun for Jennifer, as she made friends with Kristin Hahn, a producer's assistant on *Cheers* at Paramount, and to whom Jennifer would moan about her lack of success on the days when she was sure she'd never get another part again (at the time she often found herself losing parts to Kristy Swanson). She and Hahn would get together with the other Hill girls and enjoy drunken nights out where none of them were allowed to talk to guys. Hahn did, however, break this rule once, by inviting along a new male friend of hers. The Hill's resident pet dog didn't take to him, however, and bit him on the backside. The bitee was an actor called Matthew Perry.

In 1992, after being in LA for three years, Jennifer managed to snag a part on a skit comedy series entitled *The Edge*, which attempted to ape the ever-popular *Saturday Night Live* format of mixing comedy sketches together with parodies of

JENNIFER ANISTON

THE ONE WITH ALL THE STRUGGLE

TV series and adverts. Among Jennifer's co-stars was actor Alan Ruck, who, like Jennifer Grey, also appeared in the original *Ferris Bueller* movie. But while fans remember it as being something close to comic genius, the show failed to get viewers, and yet again, Jennifer found herself part of a cancelled show. This one did, at least, last a full season, though. And besides Jennifer, several of those involved went on to better things. Her co-star Wayne Knight found fame in Jerry Seinfeld's hit show *Seinfeld*, while director David Merkin moved on to a certain animated sitcom called *The Simpsons*.

It still appeared that Jennifer was going to be nowhere near that lucky. She got a small guest slot on the highly experimental sitcom *Herman's Head* in which William Ragsdale played Herman Brooks, a publisher's fact-checker and wannabe writer, who addressed the camera directly and was accompanied on-screen by a four-person Greek Chorus who revealed his inner thoughts to the audience. Too weird to attract a massive audience, it remains a cult favourite like *The Edge*, and it featured Jennifer in just two of its 72 episodes, as Suzie Brooks, Herman's little sister. But check the regular cast list, and there's another *Friends-*

related coincidence, as one of the show's regular cast members was actress Jane Sibbett, later Ross' lesbian wife Carol on *Friends*.

Jennifer also popped up opposite Scott Bakula on *Quantum Leap*, as he leapt into the body of a disabled Vietnam veteran in 1968 in the fifth season episode *Nowhere to Run: August 10, 1968*. She also guested in the disastrous two-seasons-only attempt at reviving Sixties hit *Burke's Law*, in an episode in the show's first season, called *Who Killed the Beauty Queen.*

While the TV work kept coming in more-or-less steadily, Jennifer was resolutely petrified of auditioning for films. The reason for this, she said in an interview, was because of her agent: he insisted she was better suited to the small screen and would become a TV star. "I hated him for that," she later told an interviewer ruefully, "because I thought 'you have no faith in me'."

In spite of her fear of movie auditions, in 1993, Jennifer made her big screen debut, albeit rather inauspiciously, in a film which would spawn no less than five sequels. The film was an ultra-low budget tongue-in-cheek horror flick, *Leprechaun.*

Three-foot-six Warwick Davis, who had previously starred in *Willow* and as Wicket the

JENNIFER ANISTON

THE ONE WITH ALL THE STRUGGLE

Ewok in *Return of the Jedi*, plays a leprechaun with an attitude problem who cheerfully murders anyone who gets near his gold. He's eventually outsmarted by Dan O'Grady, who steals the gold and is chased by the leprechaun back to the US. Captured by Dan, who suffers a stroke before he can kill him, the leprechaun is buried in a crate in the basement of an old house. The house is bought 10 years later by JD Reding (John Sanderford) and his sexy, spoilt daughter Tory, played by Jennifer. Needless to say, the leprechaun gets released and heads off on a murderous rampage, looking for his gold. It's up to Jennifer and three of her friends to find Dan O'Grady, who then informs them that the only thing which can destroy the leprechaun is a four-leaf clover – which they have to find before the leprechaun finishes them off.

A great work of art the movie isn't. Budgeted at just $1 million dollars, it nevertheless made a massive profit, grossing more than eight times that amount on its initial release in the US alone, and is a firm favourite with cult movie fans. Indeed sequels are still being made, with *Leprechaun 2* and *Leprechaun 3* following in 1994 and 1995, the brilliantly titled *Leprechaun 4: In Space* coming in 1996, *Leprechaun in the Hood* in

THE ONE WITH ALL THE STRUGGLE

2000 and *Leprechaun: Back 2 Tha Hood* being released in 2003. Warwick Davis returned for all of them. Needless to say, Jennifer didn't.

While Jennifer was still in a far more supportive environment than she had been while living in New York, with friends around for support, it was after filming *Leprechaun* that another incident knocked her new-found confidence. Jennifer, who weighed around 130 pounds, was told by her agent to show up for an audition wearing a leotard and tights. Jokingly, she replied that that would blow it for her. But the actual blow came when the agent told her he had, in fact, intended to ask her to lose weight, as he felt she was losing parts to actresses who better fitted the stick-thin Hollywood mould.

Still resolutely determined to make it as an actress, Jennifer began a diet and exercise regime, the nutri-system plan, and ditched her favourite snack of mayonnaise on white bread. As a result, she dropped 20 pounds in the space of 12 months. To this day, Jennifer resents being forced to become so body conscious and, in numerous interviews has spoken out against a system which equates weight with a person's value. Speaking to Susan Korones Gifford in *Redbook*, she said "I

THE ONE WITH ALL THE STRUGGLE

didn't even know I was overweight until someone told me. I hate it that your self worth is metered by how much you weigh."

Unsurprisingly, *Leprechaun* did little for Jennifer's nascent movie career. Years later, she would sideline any mention of it in interviews, telling *GQ* that "I'm confident about some things, but I'm not confident about my work" when it was mentioned. So she returned to TV, appearing briefly in a very obscure series entitled *Sunday Funnies*, before moving on to another project.

This series was yet another sitcom, entitled *Muddling Through*. But this one was built around a star, stand-up comedian Stephanie Hodge. Hodge played Connie Drego, the white-trash owner of a motel, newly released after two years in prison for shooting her cheating husband Sonny in the backside.

Attempting to pick up the pieces of her life, Connie headed back to the motel, which was being run in her absence by her eldest daughter Madeline (Jennifer), but found things complicated by Sonny continuing to live in one of the rooms, younger daughter Kerri discovering boys, and Madeline being married to the dim-witted police officer who originally arrested Connie.

JENNIFER ANISTON

THE ONE WITH ALL THE STRUGGLE

Jennifer's part was pretty much the second lead, and looked set to provide a decent showcase for her comic skills. However, true to form, things threatened to go pear-shaped pretty quickly, as the show's first episodes were recorded, then sat on the shelf while the network decided whether or not to show them. Eventually they did show them, and the series garnered adequate ratings when it appeared in July 1994. The network, CBS, wondered briefly whether or not to renew it for the new autumn season, but finally decided against doing so, largely because Hodge had moved on to another series, *Unhappily Ever After*.

In a later interview, Jennifer recalled her experiences in TV series prior to *Friends*, saying of the shows she'd appeared on before: "They've all gotten on the air except one [presumably *Sunday Funnies*, about which virtually no information seems to be available!], but they last maybe six episodes, 13 episodes, and then they are never heard of. And you think that's sort of sad. But there's a reason for it."

The fact was that if ever there *was* a reason for one of Jennifer's series to get cancelled, *Muddling Through* was the one which had it, as this time around a show she'd signed on for as a

THE ONE WITH ALL THE STRUGGLE

regular cast-member not getting renewed was really blessing in disguise. Had *Muddling Through* been picked up, Jennifer's contract would have forced her to return to it. While *Muddling Through* was sitting on the shelf, she was invited to audition for another sitcom called *Friends Like These*. And with its title shortened to just plain *Friends*, this show WAS going to get picked up for a full season that autumn. A full season and then some...

4

The one where something big happens

JENNIFER ANISTON

THE ONE WHERE SOMETHING BIG HAPPENS

The fact is that Jennifer really did come close to missing out on the part of Rachel Green in *Friends*. Not only did TV bosses only decide not to renew *Muddling Through* mere weeks before *Friends* was scheduled to begin production, but initially, Jennifer wasn't even up for the part of Rachel at all.

Friends began in 1993, when producers Marta Kauffman, David Crane and Kevin Bright pitched three sitcom ideas to production executives at NBC. Kauffman and Crane had met while studying at Brandeis University in Massachusetts. After graduation, they moved to New York and worked

THE ONE WHERE SOMETHING BIG HAPPENS

on off-Broadway musicals, before producing the highly acclaimed TV sitcom *Dream On*, where they met Kevin Bright.

The ideas for the other two shows seem to have disappeared into the mists of TV history, but the one which NBC went for as part of its 1994 autumn season, was initially going to be called *Friends Like Us*. Or *Across the Hall*. Or *Six of One*.

It was based in part on Crane and Kauffman's experiences of working in New York and of being part of a group of six friends, all in their 20s, and all with very different personalities.

As David Crane said; "We had just finished *Dream On*, which was about a guy in his 30s who had made a lot of choices in his life and was living with the consequences. We thought it would be fun to make a show about people in their 20s who were still making those choices."

As such, they also decided to break the *Dream On* mould by making the new show a TV rarity – a true ensemble piece which gave roughly equal screen time to all the characters, rather than just one, with stories focussing on their experiences as a group. Ultimately, these would be the elements which would set the show apart from its competitors and catapult it to the top of

THE ONE WHERE SOMETHING BIG HAPPENS

the viewing charts.

The characters who were to make up the show's ensemble have since, of course, become as familiar to TV viewers as their own real-life friends (sometimes more so). But all six started out as figments of Bright, Kauffman and Crane's fertile imaginations. Nominal lead was to be one Monica Geller, a chef who worked at a trendy NYC restaurant called Iridium and who had slight tendencies towards over-fastidiousness when it came to keeping things clean, tidy and in order. Backing up Monica would be her even more neurotic older brother, Ross, a married paleontologist whose pregnant wife left him for another woman; Ross' best friend, the wisecracking Chandler Bing, who lived in the apartment across the hall from Monica with his flatmate; the nice-but-dim ladies' man and not-very-talented actor Joey Tribbiani. Also in the picture was Monica's former flatmate, ditzy masseuse/folk singer Phoebe Buffay, whose life had been coloured by the absolute heights of tragedy and comedy. And last, but not least, there was Rachel Green, Monica's slightly spoilt, slightly bitchy, high school friend (and the object of Ross' unrequited love), who arrived in the pilot episode clad in a wet wedding dress, having just ditched

THE ONE WHERE SOMETHING BIG HAPPENS

her orthodontist fiancee at the altar, deciding that there had to be more to life than marriage and a life in the suburbs. Rachel took up residence in Monica's spare room, got a job waiting tables at the gang's favourite hangout, coffee shop "Central Perk". The result was instant magic.

With all the characters firmly in place in their minds, the producers set about finding the right actors to bring them to life. The search wasn't easy, as countless actors read for the parts. Describing the search for the *Friends* as "a long and hard affair", David Crane said in an interview that they saw more than a thousand applicants for each role, and often thought that the series would never get cast.

"It wasn't as if we saw eight guys who could play Chandler or six girls who were right for Phoebe, and picked the best one," he said.

In the event, it would prove easier to find the male component of the sextet, with the first role to be cast being that of Ross. "We knew how good David Schwimmer was because he had auditioned for a project we'd done the year before, so he was at the forefront all the time for Ross," David Crane said.

In spite of citing the lack of viable Chandlers as one of the most frustrating parts of the casting

THE ONE WHERE SOMETHING BIG HAPPENS

search, Crane and Kauffman also knew Matthew Perry, who had had such a painful run-in with Jennifer's dog years earlier. He almost didn't even get to read for the part, however, as he was in a similar situation to Jennifer's, having just starred in another TV pilot. If it got picked up, he would not be able to take the part of Chandler, if it were offered to him.

"To be honest, we also thought Chandler would be a relatively easy role to cast, with its load of jokes and wisecracks," Crane said. "But when we couldn't find anyone we liked, we finally asked Matthew to audition and he was the only person who made Chandler Bing come alive"

Similarly, suitable Phoebes seemed to be thin on the ground until Lisa Kudrow, already a recurring guest star on another hit New York-set sitcom, *Mad About You* (something which would be worked into the *Friends* plot, as Phoebe became the twin of Ursula, Lisa's *Mad About You* character). Crane has remembered thinking of her as the perfect Phoebe as soon as she walked into the audition, but Kudrow remembers having to return for three callbacks before being offered the part.

Casting Kudrow meant the producers were halfway there, with three roles left unfilled: Monica,

THE ONE WHERE SOMETHING BIG HAPPENS

Rachel and Joey. David Crane thought he had the perfect actress in mind for the part of Jewish American Princess Rachel – an actress called Courteney Cox. And they were also keen on another actress for the part of Monica – Jennifer Aniston.

Cox, however, had other ideas. She pleaded with Crane to be allowed to read for Monica, while Jennifer was undecided, liking both the Monica and Rachel parts, and very nearly going for Monica. Cox, however, nailed the part of Monica so perfectly, she snagged the role, which, in the event, worked fine for Jennifer, who had decided she would rather go with being Rachel. "I was torn between reading for Rachel and Monica", Aniston says, "but Rachel felt right. Two hours after I'd read for Rachel, the producers rang me at home and said it was a done deal, and I was beyond thrilled." The producers were also thrilled, feeling they'd truly found an actress who could make Rachel at once spoilt and clueless about how to get along in the real world, yet adorable with it.

The final 'Friend', Joey, was filled by Matt LeBlanc. Crane admits to having had another actor in mind for the part, but was won over by LeBlanc's take on the struggling actor with an

THE ONE WHERE SOMETHING BIG HAPPENS

eye for the girls. Of the six, only Courteney Cox had had anything even approaching major success in the entertainment industry, having been a teen model, appearing in two Bruce Springsteen videos and numerous TV and cinema movies, including *Ace Ventura: Pet Detective* as well as enjoying a stint on another hugely successful sitcom, *Family Ties*, as Michael J Fox's character's girlfriend. LeBlanc, like Jennifer, had been in a couple of TV shows which went nowhere, including an unsuccessful spinoff from the smash-hit *Married With Children*, entitled *Top of the Heap*. Perry had also done a few films, TV movies and big screen outings, his best-known film role being that of River Phoenix's best friend in *A Night in the Life of Jimmy Reardon*. Schwimmer, meanwhile, soon to be the man who with Jennifer would be part of TV's most eagerly watched will-they-won't-they couple, had done a few features and enjoyed brief stints on *NYPD Blue* and *The Wonder Years*.

With the six leads finally in place the producers had only one worry left – that they wouldn't have the right chemistry. It was a concern which went right out the window as soon as the actors first got together. It was, the produc-

THE ONE WHERE SOMETHING BIG HAPPENS

ers said later, as if they genuinely had known and hung out with each other for years.

The pilot, scripted by Kauffman and Crane themselves, and directed by TV veteran James Burrows, was shot on the Warner Brothers lot in summer 1994. Immediately after the pilot wrapped, Jennifer found herself joining the others back in front of the camera for another bit of filming, however – the now-legendary title scene, which featured all six of the *Friends* dancing around a fountain.

The sequence took a few hours to shoot, and was filmed after the pilot so that the actors would at least feel that they knew each other a little bit. The water in the fountain was heated, in an attempt to prevent the actors from freezing – a measure which didn't entirely work as it cooled off quickly.

The other component of the title sequence, the theme song *I'll be There For You.* composed and performed by pop group Rembrandts, had yet to be written or recorded, and Marta Crane later remembered that the cast were actually dancing around to "some kind of funky soul thing." The fountain-dancing sequence was initially intended to play out uninterrupted under the credits, but in

THE ONE WHERE SOMETHING BIG HAPPENS

the event, it would do this only in the pilot episode, as one of the few changes the network wanted made was to this sequence, which executives felt "locked the viewer out" as the *Friends* looked to be having too much fun, and not letting the folks at home in on it. So for its eventual use, the sequence was edited with shots taken from episodes throughout the series.

After which, everybody went home to wait and see what the network had to say. It was a tense time, but the news was good. NBC loved the show. They sent the cast on an all-expenses-paid bonding trip to Las Vegas as a thank-you, and, after the title was finally shortened to just plain *Friends*, the show was in business.

US viewers got their first glimpse of Jennifer as Rachel on 22 September 1994 (British viewers had to wait just over six months longer, until 28 April 1995). The show was an immediate hit, with one NBC executive saying it had "pretty much been a dreamboat ride. Friends is a bona fide hit and a water-cooler show every Friday morning.We wanted to be in business with Kauffman, Bright and Crane, and we were very interested in doing a show that looked at this age group. So we had confidence."

THE ONE WHERE SOMETHING BIG HAPPENS

Setting itself apart from everything else on the air, the show managed the unthinkable – while nominally labelled a "Generation X" series, it appealed to viewers across the board. Initially, the "Gen X" label worried Crane, who said "We were a little stunned" with all the Gen-X labels attached to the show, particularly as he and Kaufmann had based it in part on a time in their lives which had taken place long before the "Generation X" catchphrase had been invented.

Whatever the case, this was good news at last for Jennifer, whose hard work and struggles had finally paid off. And it seemed that it had paid off for her almost before it paid off for any of the others, as Rachel quickly became the viewers' darling for the first season. Eventually, all the cast members would get a season of the show which would be "theirs", in terms of which of them was the favourite of those watching at home (the writers kept the ensemble balance going at all times, never favouring one character with more screen time, or storylines than another.)

But Rachel seemed first to carve her name into the pop culture zeitgeist. Indeed, she gets most of the best scenes in the pilot, bursting into Central Perk in her wedding dress, and ending

THE ONE WHERE SOMETHING BIG HAPPENS

the episode by choosing to move in with Monica – while reigniting Ross' passions for her along the way. The Ross 'n' Rachel storyline would become the lynchpin of the show's first season, and indeed, would generate its first season-finale cliffhanger, when Rachel found out about Ross' feelings for her, and went to meet him at the airport, only to find that while on a business trip, he'd met an old colleague and started an affair with her. It was the first of many twists in the duo's relationship.

Above and beyond the Ross 'n' Rachel thing, however, there was one other element of the show's first season which would give Jennifer an even bigger share of the limelight: her hairstyle. Created almost by accident, when her hairdresser tried razor-cutting her hair into what became initially known as the "shag" and later as the "Rachel", Jennifer's layered hairstyle, which curved in, framing her face, became the most-copied in the country. Jennifer herself at first claimed to hate the cut, and wanted to wear a hat until she was given permission by show supremos to change it. But so great was its success, that she was persuaded to keep it, as everyone from the woman on the street to the

THE ONE WHERE SOMETHING BIG HAPPENS

characters of other shows like *Beverly Hills 90210* all adopted the cut.

Friends finished its first season on a massive high. Reviews were great, viewing figures were high, and everybody loved Jennifer, who was fully solvent as well, thanks to her $35,000-an-episode salary. And things would only get better.

5

The one where
Jennifer hits
the big time

JENNIFER ANISTON

THE ONE WHERE JENNIFER HITS THE BIG TIME

When somebody follows you 20 blocks to the pharmacy, where they watch you buy toilet paper, you know your life has changed," said Jennifer Aniston in 1997.

And indeed, by 1997, thanks to the success of *Friends*, Jennifer's life had changed out of all proportion. In fact, it had changed out of all proportion even before the first 1994-95 season had ended. Not only was there the haircut, but there were magazine covers, interviews, and the paparazzi, a pack of people with whom Jennifer would begin a running battle as soon as she found fame, and who have continued to dog her

THE ONE WHERE JENNIFER HITS THE BIG TIME

until the present day.

On-screen, Jennifer's storylines dominated the first season of the sitcom, as Rachel discovered how to do laundry, had her heart broken by an Italian stallion she met during a power cut, didn't get hired by Saks as an assistant buyer, and almost got back together with ex-fiancee Barry. And throughout it all, she remained cheerfully oblivious to the fact that Ross was madly in love with her. Until the end of the first season, that is, when thanks to a slip of Chandler's tongue, a birthday gift from Ross took on more significance than any of the characters at first thought, leading up to that cliffhanger season-finale.

Numerous critics predicted that the end of the "Rachel doesn't know Ross likes her" storyline would bring about the end of the series, especially as the two swiftly became an item in the second season. Needless to say, they were wrong, as the comedy swiftly became one of the first shows to manage to evade falling apart as it got two of its lead characters together.

And as the show grew in popularity, so too did Jennifer's bank balance – which would continue to grow steadily as the show went on. Like the others, she had started the show on "scale", about

THE ONE WHERE JENNIFER HITS THE BIG TIME

$22,500 per episode. This had swiftly risen to around $35,000, but by 1996, when the sextet had three years of their original five-year contracts left to go, they were asking for $100,000 per episode, in the wake of network NBC's announcement of a $4-million-per-episode syndication deal for the series, contingent on the show running for five years.

Aware that the network couldn't have cemented the deal without them, and that it wouldn't be able to fulfil the five-year criteria if any of them left, the stars first negotiated as a team, then, when that didn't work, separately, leaving their individual agents to thrash out deals for each of them.

There was even a suggestion that unless NBC came up with more than the $75,000 per episode "compromise" offer it initially made, the *Friends* would go on strike. The suggestion was quickly refuted by the actors, who all showed up on schedule to read through the new scripts on the first day of season three production. In the event, the cast agreed to go with the $75,000 per episode deal, with proviso for incremental increases over the show's next few seasons. Like the others, Jennifer also received a $200,000 Christmas bonus in December 1996, which NBC hoped would keep

THE ONE WHERE JENNIFER HITS THE BIG TIME

any threats of industrial action at bay. From there on in, the incremental raises would keep on kicking in, as Jennifer's pay went from $75,000 to $100,000 to $125,000 by the 2000 season. At which point the contracts were up again, and the cast asked for, and got, an unheard of $750,000 each per episode. Two years later, that went to an even-more-unheard-of $1 million per episode. All of which meant that Jennifer could indulge her passion for houses and antiques even more.

At the point of the first salary dispute, *Friends* was ranked fourth overall in the US ratings, and had become a UK hit on Channel 4. Tie-in books, T-shirts and other merchandising were already raking in a fortune, and the award nominations were rolling in as well, with two consecutive Golden Globe nominations for Best TV Comedy already under the show's belt, and more to come. There were, however, plenty of by-products of fame which Jennifer could well have done without, including having her face plastered on to the packaging of a brand of Russian condoms, the pictures illegally cribbed from the famous issue of *Rolling Stone* which featured her nearly nude on the cover. Not all bad though as That Hairstyle did get her a highly lucrative contract as

JENNIFER ANISTON

the face (and hair!) of L'Oreal Elvive shampoo, which put her in even more magazines and on more TV screens worldwide, spouting the shampoo's catchphrase "Because you're worth it!"

With *Friends* riding high, Jennifer also seemed to have conquered her fear of auditioning for the big screen. In fact, almost as soon as the series started, she and the other five began trying to turn the show's success into film careers.

After making a quick appearance alongside Matthew Perry in a rather bizarre video guide to Microsoft's Windows 95, Jennifer's first film appearance since *Leprechaun* came with the 1996 indie *Dream for an Insomniac*.

Jennifer didn't even play the lead. Rather, she appeared as the best friend of Ione Skye, who played a woman unable to find a boyfriend due to the impossibly high standard she sets for all potentials. When she eventually meets Mackenzie Astin, with whom she clicks, she's dismayed to find he already has a girlfriend. But certain that she will win him in the end, she grabs Jennifer's character and moves to Los Angeles in pursuit of him.

The reviews for the film, while generally positive, weren't overwhelming. Neither was its reception at the box office. Jennifer, however,

THE ONE WHERE JENNIFER HITS THE BIG TIME

received none of the usual backlash reserved for stars of the small-screen who try to do movies, even though most critics seemed to agree that she didn't do much beyond looking pretty and sporting her famous hairdo.

Of her *Friends* co-stars, by this point only Courteney Cox had had any real success in films, with the *Scream* horror movies. But, perhaps mindful of *Leprechaun*, Jennifer seemed set on making the romantic comedy her genre of choice in her attempts to make it as a movie star. Her next effort, however, would be rather more of a starry affair, as she joined the ensemble cast of writer/actor/director Edward Burns' *She's The One*.

She's The One was Burns' follow-up to his surprise hit *The Brothers McMullen*, a film to which it was unfavourably compared as being rather too similar. In Burns' second story about the trials and tribulations of Irish-American brothers, Jennifer played Renée Fitzpatrick, wife of Francis (Mike McGlone). In the film's subsidiary plotline, Francis is cheating on Renée with Heather (Cameron Diaz). Starring alongside Jennifer was another refugee from a hit NBC sitcom, John Mahoney, better known as Kelsey Grammer's father on *Frasier*.

Besides the absurdity of anyone wanting to

THE ONE WHERE JENNIFER HITS THE BIG TIME

cheat on Jennifer (even with Cameron Diaz), the film seemed to go down fairly well generally, although again, it wasn't a smash-hit or anything even approaching the sort of movie Jennifer would need to truly launch herself on to the big screen. But then, as she played only a secondary role, perhaps it wasn't meant to be, but rather intended as something to help her get her feet a little wetter before taking on a leading role.

Jennifer's schedule had been exhausting on *She's The One*. True, she wasn't the lead, but she had to film her scenes back-to-back with *Friends* episodes, working on the movie every weekend. For her debut as a movie's leading lady, she'd wait until the show was on a break from filming, squeezing in the shooting of 1997's *Picture Perfect* when there was no Rachel to get in the way.

Picture Perfect was, you guessed it, another romantic comedy, with rather more emphasis on the comedy than any of Jennifer's movies thus far. Jennifer played Kate Mosley, a woman with the sort of career that Rachel (at that point anyway) could only dream about. Kate is a junior advertising executive at a New York advertising firm. Designer-clad and determined, Kate was hell-bent on making it to the top, but found that being single was

THE ONE WHERE JENNIFER HITS THE BIG TIME

blocking her way. So to impress the boss, she invents a fictional boyfriend, Nick, who works wonders. Not only does he boost her career, but he piques the jealousy of Kate's co-worker Sam (Kevin Bacon), in whom Kate has had an unnoticed romantic interest for a while. Trouble, however, ensues when Kate actually has to produce a flesh-and-blood Nick at office gatherings, and hires an actor (Jay Mohr) to play him. Even more trouble ensues when he actually falls for Kate for real.

Light as the proverbial feather, *Picture Perfect* was, yet again, received lukewarmly by the critics and viewing public. Frustratingly for Jennifer, it seemed that her developing film career was becoming a slightly more successful re-run of her previous attempts at breaking into TV.

And so, as *Friends* became an ever-more-unstoppable juggernaut of success, Jennifer pressed on with the movies, reverting to a supporting best-friend role, with *Til There Was You*, in which she was BF to Jeanne Tripplehorn, aiding and abetting her in a relationship with childhood friend Dylan McDermott. The poster tagline stated that it took Tripplehorn and McDermott "20 years to fall in love at first sight", and with yet another ho-hum rom-com under her

THE ONE WHERE JENNIFER HITS THE BIG TIME

belt, it must have felt as if it was going to take at least that long for Jennifer to get a hit movie, as her thunder was stolen this time round by another supporting player, ironically also the star of a New York-set sitcom: one Sarah Jessica Parker, in the showy role of an outrageous former child star.

Nevertheless, Jennifer was still undaunted. And so she signed on for yet another big screen romantic comedy, *The Object of My Affection*, this time back in a leading role, and with (a slightly darker script than any of her previous films.

This time round, Jennifer played Nina, yet another single career girl, who meets and becomes fast friends with George (Paul Rudd, who would eventually become a recurring player on *Friends'* final season, where his character would wind up wed to Phoebe), after being introduced to him at a party. The two move in together, but it's a coupling with a twist – their relationship is platonic as George is gay. Nina swiftly becomes pregnant by her no-good boyfriend, dumps him, and asks George to raise the baby with her. But then she realises she's falling for him, and things get even more complicated when he gets a new boyfriend.

Exhibiting shades of the later Madonna/Rupert Everett's *The Next Best Thing*, *The Object of My*

THE ONE WHERE JENNIFER HITS THE BIG TIME

Affection did at least stand out from the pack of standard-issue, cookie-cutter romantic comedies. But once again, it failed to set the box office alight, and Jennifer was still a TV star. A massive TV star, true, but not a movie name. Not yet.

She was, however, pretty happy. She had banked a $3-million-fee for *Picture Perfect*, and had left her days of communal living behind her, in real life, if not on the small screen. Her newfound financial security had allowed her to purchase a hilltop house with a fantastic view over Los Angeles, a private gym, tiled bathroom and all the other amenities expected of a swanky Hollywood hideaway. Finally able to splash out, she filled it to the brim with antique furniture. She was also winning plaudits from within the industry (and, it should be noted, none of the critics had ever savaged any of her movie performances, even if they hadn't exactly lauded them), with the likes of Glen Gordon Caron, veteran creator of hit series *Moonlighting* and director of *Picture Perfect*, lauding her ability to inject humanity into a scene as well as comedic timing. "On some level, everything Jennifer does as an actor has to be with the business of being a human being," he told *US* magazine. "What makes her special isn't peculiar to youth. I could see her working into her 60s."

On *Friends*, Ross and Rachel had got together, split up, got back together and split up again ad nauseam. But the audience showed no sign of getting fed up with it, and even as the other characters' relationships – including the shock romance between Courteney Cox's Monica and Matthew Perry's Chandler – moved in on Ross 'n' Rachel's turf, nobody ever suggested that they were taking a backseat.

And equally certainly, nobody was getting fed up with reading about Jennifer's off-screen love-life either. A source of much gossip and speculation ever since *Friends* had hit big, this was one area which was about to get a whole lot more interesting.

6

The one with the
fairy tale romance

JENNIFER ANISTON

THE ONE WITH THE FAIRY TALE ROMANCE

As with any celebrity, Jennifer's love-life had been speculated on, rumoured about, inspected and dissected from the very second she first hit the spotlight.

Among those she's been linked to are actor Charlie Schlatter, her on-screen brother in the *Ferris Bueller* sitcom, and actor Daniel MacDonald. Also on the list is Adam Duritz, lead singer of the band Counting Crows, who adds a bit of *Friends*-incest to the proceedings, having also dated Courteney Cox.

However, up until 1998, Jennifer had had only one high(ish) profile relationship, with actor

JENNIFER ANISTON

THE ONE WITH THE FAIRY TALE ROMANCE

Tate Donovan. Donovan had first risen to prominence in the wartime drama *Memphis Belle*, although he'd been making TV appearances since his teens. He and Jennifer met in November 1995, and quickly became an item. Donovan had previously dated Hollywood star Sandra Bullock, after meeting her on the set of their comedy *Love Potion Number 9*, and one (false) tabloid report had Jennifer stealing Donovan from Bullock, then having an all-out catfight with the *Speed* star over him.

At the time he started seeing Jennifer, Donovan was starring in the sitcom *Partners*, alongside Jon Cryer, who had once been the favourite to play Chandler Bing. With *Friends* helmsman James Burrows taking directing duties on some of the episodes, *Partners* was (like countless other series) mooted as "the new *Friends*". Unfortunately, it lasted only 22 episodes before being cancelled by the Fox network. Donovan then found more success as the voice of *Hercules* in Disney's cartoon about the legendary Greek hero. In 1998, with speculation rife that the couple were headed down the aisle, he guested on five episodes of *Friends* as Joshua, a crush of Rachel's. But the relationship was already on the

THE ONE WITH THE FAIRY TALE ROMANCE

rocks and the couple parted in April 1998.

At the time, the split was blamed on Donovan's reluctance to propose. However, he later told *In Touch* magazine that the pair ended their relationship because they were simply "different people." And Aniston's trademark ambition didn't mesh well with his laid-back look on life.

"She likes top-notch hotels and luxury, and I like bed-and-breakfasts and riding my bike. That's the most shallow version of it, but it's indicative of our personalities." Donovan told the magazine. He later returned to Fox, finding success as part of the hit teen soap *The OC*.

But Jennifer didn't have much time to mope over Donovan, as there was a new, and ultimately very exciting romance in the offing. With none other than A-list Hollywood celebrity Brad Pitt.

In 1998, Pitt was already a huge movie star with the likes of *A River Runs Through It, Legends of the Fall* and *Seven* in his back catalogue to prove it. He was also the veteran of a string of high-profile romances with some of moviedom's sexiest leading ladies. Pitt's list of exes dwarfed Jennifer's and included such luminaries as Robin Givens, Juliette Lewis and fellow A-lister Gwyneth

THE ONE WITH THE FAIRY TALE ROMANCE

Paltrow, with whom he was engaged.

Like much of their courtship, Brad and Jennifer's first meeting was shrouded in secrecy, and sources differ on how their initial dinner date was actually arranged. But legend has it that Brad saw Jennifer on *Friends*, which he later claimed to be a fan of prior to ever meeting her, and arranged an introduction, although whether this was through friends, or through their respective publicists remains a moot point.

Clearly, he had the right idea, however, as Jennifer would later say that she knew the couple were right for each other from the moment they met. In an interview with German magazine *Amica*, she told the interviewer "When we met it was there right away – that first date spark. It was clear that we were right for each other." Although she also said that Brad wasn't typical of the kind of guy she usually went for, claiming that she preferred "quirky guys who were a bit different and not the really obviously good-looking guys."

Jennifer's assertion that they were perfect for each other was seconded by the couple's friends, including director James Gray, who told *People* magazine that the duo even finished each other's sentences. During a meal he had with them, he

THE ONE WITH THE FAIRY TALE ROMANCE

said that Brad was then in the middle of trying to quit smoking. "Jennifer was telling him to wear his patch," Gray told the magazine "She's trying to get him not to smoke, but she smokes. He says, 'Don't smoke either, honey!'" and she says, 'Well you quit first!' They're perfect together."

Wary of the press after his high-profile relationship with Paltrow, Brad and Jennifer were determined to keep their relationship as secret as possible, shrouding it in as much mystery as they could in an attempt to keep it away from the prying eyes of the cameras. This on-going battle would continue even after their eventual wedding: when the couple bought his-and-hers Range Rovers, Brad's was reportedly specially equipped with a rear-facing camera, linked to a database of paparazzi's number-plates, so that he could be alerted whenever he was being followed.

Nevertheless, rumours that they were seeing each other went through the gossip press like wildfire, and it seemed almost too good to be true: the star of TV's most popular sitcom, and one of Hollywood's biggest movie stars were in love. Photographers were offered six-figure sums to get a picture of them together.

And then, finally, at the 1998 Free Tibet

THE ONE WITH THE FAIRY TALE ROMANCE

concert in Washington DC, Hollywood's hottest couple made it official with a public embrace on their balcony, a kiss which was photographed and shown round the world as the question on everyone's lips changed. It had been "Are they together?" Now it was "When are they getting married?"

Having been in no hurry whatsoever to answer the first question, Brad and Jennifer certainly weren't rushing to answer the second. There was plenty for the tabloids to feast on in the meantime though, including reports that Pitt was ripping apart and remodelling the Sixties Hollywood Hills mansion he'd shared with Paltrow to make it more Jennifer-friendly, with workmen working round the clock to install a bath which would comfortably fit two. Elsewhere, Jennifer revisited her sketch comedy past, and appeared on *Saturday Night Live*, where she took part in comedy skits which spoofed both the paparazzi who hounded her and Brad, and one Athena Marie Rolando, Brad's notorious stalker.

7

The one with the wedding

JENNIFER ANISTON

THE ONE WITH THE WEDDING

As summer 2000 reached its heights, and speculation that the duo were to wed any day hit fever pitch, an arrest warrant was issued for Athena Marie Rolando, who in 1999 had broken into Pitt's house and was found there by police, wearing his clothes and clutching a note which apologised to him for wrecking his romance with Paltrow by putting a curse on it. On 21 July, reports were rife in the press that the very next weekend, Brad and Jennifer would marry at a Malibu mansion.

Brad's publicist Cindy Guagenti was quick to pour cold water on the story, however, telling

THE ONE WITH THE WEDDING

anyone who asked that the two wouldn't be heading for the altar "in the near future."

She did hint that they might marry within the year, but also told press that she had to stamp out a wedding rumour "every two weeks."

In the event, just six days later, Guagenti changed tack and confirmed that the wedding was on, set for 29 July 2000.

The few recent leaks notwithstanding, Brad and Jennifer had done an amazing job of keeping the wedding secret, especially given the lavish affair it would eventually turn out to be. With a price tag estimated at $1 million, the wedding featured 200 guests, including countless celebrities, 50,000 flowers, four bands, an entire gospel choir and fireworks priced at more than $20,000 alone. Part of California's Pacific Coast Highway was closed down briefly, much to the annoyance of locals, and steps were taken to make sure that no flying paparazzi got any helicopter shots, with a federal official on hand to make sure that the airspace over the Malibu clifftop didn't become too crowded with camera-bearing choppers – the airspace immediately above the property was declared an official no-fly zone. The clifftop itself was part of a five-acre compound the couple rented

JENNIFER ANISTON

THE ONE WITH THE WEDDING

for the day from producer Marcy Carsey (famous for *Roseanne* and *The Cosby Show*). It took an entire army of workers to ready the place for the nuptials, erecting tents, hanging lanterns and setting up a canopied bridal walkway (much of which was designed to hide the ceremony from flying paparazzi). The flowers were provided by the famed La Premiere of Beverly Hills, who set the tables with roses, wisteria and tulips before floating lotus flowers on the specially-built fountain. Brad, according to one worker speaking in *People* magazine later, had asked for the "Zen garden look" and Jennifer had wanted "tons of candles". Presumably both were more than happy, then, with the brown sugar Thai candles which lit up the reception tent.

For several months, Jennifer had been sporting a Silvia Damiani wedding ring, reportedly co-designed by Pitt, who had worked with the jeweller for months to get the style just right, and the ceremony would be literally drenched in designer-labels, and would feature more of Damiani's work, as the Italian jeweller provided two white gold wedding bands, Brad's embedded with ten diamonds and engraved with the inscription "Jen 2000", and Jennifer's similarly engraved

THE ONE WITH THE WEDDING

with "Brad 2000" along with 20 diamonds.

The bride wore a floor-length white gown by Milan-based, ex-Prada designer Lawrence Steele, teamed with custom-made ivory suede high-heels by Manolo Blahnik. Steele also provided pale green slip-style dresses for the bridesmaids, actress Andrea Bendewald, and documentarian Kristin Hahn-Singer, and cream silk outfits for Jennifer's flower girls, who showered her with petals and blew bubbles. Her circular veil was topped off by a crown interlaced with pearls and Swarovski crystal. Jennifer had, apparently, directed that her outfit was to be "sexy-but-pretty" and finished it off by carrying a bouquet of Dutch roses. The groom and best man (Pitt's brother Doug) wore a tuxedo by Hedi Slimane and a Prada suit respectively. Prior to the ceremony, the happy couple had had matching blonde highlights done at the posh Beverly Hills Canale Salon, and Jennifer's hair was then styled by Chris McMillan, he who had created the infamous "Rachel" cut. *Friends* make-up artist Robin Siegel did her make-up.

In spite of all the expense, however, the wedding was not without its lighter moments, as the best man dropped the ring and Jennifer and Brad included vows they'd written themselves in

THE ONE WITH THE WEDDING

the ceremony, with Pitt promising to "split the difference on the thermostat." And Jennifer vowing in return that she would keep on making his "favourite banana milkshake." She also gave the guests a show of Rachel-style comic timing, by missing her cue on another part of the ceremony, and then blurting out that she'd "never done this before!"

Giving Jennifer away was her father John, while faces in the congregation included all Jennifer's *Friends* cast-mates except Matt LeBlanc, who was in Budapest to film *All the King's Men*, David Schwimmer's girlfriend, the sexy Israeli actress Mili Avital, Edward Norton, Pitt's *Fight Club* co-star, Salma Hayek, Cameron Diaz, Kathy Najimy and David Spade. Much was made of the fact that one person not in attendance was the bride's mother, Nancy, with the press blaming her absence variously on comments she had made about Jennifer's hair on television and a tell-all book she had recently written.

While guests later maintained that the whole affair was as un-showbiz-like as it could possibly be, the complexity of the arrangements ensured that it had numerous elements which most weddings probably wouldn't have featured. Behind

THE ONE WITH THE WEDDING

the smokescreen, guests had initially been told of the plans (and sworn to secrecy) several weeks earlier, and invitations had been sent by post. Following instructions, and with precision usually only seen in high-level espionage operations, they had initially congregated at the nearby Malibu High School, before getting into minivan shuttles to be driven the five miles to the wedding site. All staff had to sign contracts which stipulated that if they talked to the press, they would be liable for fines of up to $100,000.

On arrival, the guests drank iced tea and punch while the string quartet serenaded them with classical pieces, before taking their seats for the service, which finally began at 6.30pm, as Jennifer walked down the aisle to a six-piece band performing *Love is the Greatest Thing*.

In the event, it all went off without a hitch – well, except for the actual getting hitched part. And one minor lawsuit surrounding the ring, which the couple filed shortly after the wedding against Damiani International. Brad and Jennifer claimed that the company had agreed that they would never attempt to reproduce the wedding bands made for the couple (or Jennifer's engagement ring) but had done so anyway, selling "Brad

Jennifer Aniston (2nd right) with the cast of 'Friends'. The show ran for 10 years with the last episode being shown in the USA in May, 2004. The show has won numerous awards and here we see the gang collecting another Emmy to add to the collection. Pictured left to right: David Schwimmer (Ross), Lisa Kudrow (Pheobe), Matthew Perry (Chandler), Courtney Cox-Arquette (Monica), Jennifer Aniston (Rachel), Matt LeBlanc (Joey),

Jennifer as a cashier in the comedy drama film 'The Good Girl' (2002). Jennifer garnered rave reviews from the critics for her gutsy performance.

Jennifer Aniston has ranked highly as one of the sexiest women in the world in numerous polls.

Jennifer Aniston and Brad Pitt married in 2000. The wedding was a lavish affair and guests included Edward Norton, Salma Hayek, Cameron Diaz and of course, most of the cast of 'Friends'.

THE ONE WITH THE WEDDING

and Jennifer" rings of 18 karat white or yellow gold, and featuring either 12 or 13 diamonds, to the public at large priced at $1000 each. In the event, like the wedding itself, the lawsuit had a happy ending, however, with the jewellry company issuing a statement in 2002 saying the proceedings had been "amicably resolved" and were the result of an "unfortunate misunderstanding."

JENNIFER ANISTON

THE ONE WITH THE WEDDING

Spotlight on Brad Pitt...

Any golden girl needs a golden boy and there's no one quite so blessed with 24 carat looks and career than Brad Pitt. Born on 18 December 1963, Pitt was brought up in Springfield, Missouri where he would begin to show his desire to be noticed in school – after all, Pitt was voted Best Dressed Student in the Kickapoo High School Yearbook and would leave audiences of his peers somewhat stunned when he and his chums would dress up as 'The Brief Boys'; well, 'dress up' is probably an overstatement actually as the group would perform Beach Boys songs with self-penned lyrics in nothing but their underpants.

His time at the frat house Chi at University of Missouri proved to be no different as Pitt thrilled the local female populace by appearing in the student calendar *Men of Mizzou* (posing proudly with his torso on display) and taking a turn as a male stripper in a charity strip show – such saucy turns though would be played down Pitt later: "One time I was at university and they did this cheesy calendar on campus," he jokingly recalled in an interview. "They had a little party for all the people who were featured on it. I arrived and said, "I'm supposed to check in, I'm Brad Pitt." And the girl at the door's face fell. She just went, "Oh..." She obviously has [had] some vision of me as being this six-foot-four Italian guy. She just couldn't believe it."

While she may have been non-plussed (and perhaps in urgent need of a white stick), Pitt's days at uni were numbered after he was involved in a serious car crash. Thankfully escaping unhurt, Pitt soon realised though that his journalism course was simply not satisfying his creative urges and two days before graduating - and a mere two points shy of getting his degree - Pitt got into his car 'Runaround Sue' and headed for the Hollywood Hills. While Pitt would do down the atypical struggling actor route by working in a variety of menial jobs such as dressing up as a big yellow chicken to promote a fast food restaurant and driving strippers to and from bachelor parties, the young Hollywood wannabe would go on to get bit parts in shows such as *Dallas*, *Thirtysomething* and *21 Jump Street* (alongside Johnny Depp) and make his mark in TV movies such as *A Stoning In Fulham County* and *Too Young To Die?*

While Pitt made his feature film debut in ham horror spoof *Cutting Class*, Pitt's real big

THE ONE WITH THE WEDDING

screen breakthrough came when he appeared as JD in the hit movie *Thelma And Louise*. Telling the story of two women on the run, his part was small but perfectly formed as he played the sultry JD who shows Geena Davis's character Thelma exactly what she had been missing in the bedroom department for all her married life. Before, of course, making off with the women's savings.

His turn wowed audiences and Pitt was soon being eyed up by the power mongers in Tinseltown as a potential young star-in-waiting. While his next three films would fare less well at the box office – *The Favor*, *Johnny Suede* and *Cool World* – Pitt eventually took on the role of Paul Maclean in the Robert Redford-helmed *A River Runs Through It* which would end up with critics hailing him as the new - surprise, surprise - Robert Redford.

Always one for ripping up any labels that people try and slap on him, Pitt would then shock his growing base of fans by playing the serial killer Early Grayce in *Kalifornia*. Sporting greasy hair, a shabby beard and serious sinus problems, the monster that Pitt created not only utterly convinced critics that here was a great actor in the making but it also enabled Pitt to maul his emerging Robert Redford image; a pretty boy

THE ONE WITH THE WEDDING

persona which Pitt would then happily poke fun at when he appeared as Floyd the hunky stoner in *True Romance*.

His turn as Tristan Ludlow in *Legends Of The Fall* would see Pitt finally establish himself as a true star as he chewed scenery alongside acting legend Anthony Hopkins. And managed to end up arguing with the director Edward Zwick over the shooting schedule – an incident that reportedly resulted in furniture being thrown across the set.

Tantrums aside, Pitt went on to score another box office hit as the moribund blood sucker Louis de Pointe du Lac in *Interview With A Vampire* starring alongside Tom Cruise but it was in 1995 that Pitt the superstar was finally born when he played Detective David Mills in *Seven*, a dark, gruelling thriller about two cops on the trail of a twisted serial killer.

While some of Pitt's female fans were horrified by the film's pitch-black nature, it would cement in the eyes of the Hollywood studios that this guy was not only box office gold but could also deliver powerhouse performances on a regular basis – something that was further underlined when Pitt landed himself a Golden Globe and an Oscar nomination for his next role as Jeffrey Goines in

JENNIFER ANISTON

THE ONE WITH THE WEDDING

Terry Gilliam's sci-fi classic *Twelve Monkeys*.

While Pitt's subsequent films would go on to flounder with movies such as the controversial *Devil's Own* and *Seven Years In Tibet*, he would confound his critics when he played the punch drunk, 'soap' salesman Tyler Durden in the 90's iconic flick *Fight Club* - a role which he has often been quoted as saying is his career best.

In recent years, Pitt has gone on to reaffirm his position as one of Hollywood's greats with roles in films such as *Ocean's Eleven* and *Troy* and he's also shocked fans with his announcement that he plans to become an architect - or to be more precise, to serve an informal apprenticeship with Frank Gehry, one of the world's most acclaimed architects.

Perhaps more importantly, Pitt has of course finally met and married the woman of his dreams, Jennifer Aniston. After all, perhaps unsurprisingly, Pitt's love life has garnered more column inches in the press than his career. While linked with many leading ladies over the years, his previous long term serious relationships have ultimately failed – back in the late eighties, Pitt had a three-year relationship with actress Juliette Lewis after they fell for each other on the set of the TV movie *Too*

JENNIFER ANISTON

THE ONE WITH THE WEDDING

Young To Die? The relationship, though, ground to a halt after Lewis became a little too enamoured with Scientology and her supposed plans for marriage.

Then of course there was Gwyneth Paltrow. The two would meet on the set of *Seven* with Pitt saying that he fell in love with her at first sight while Paltrow would quip that it was actually on second sight for her - because she'd already fallen head over heels with Pitt when she saw him in *Thelma And Louise*.

The ensuing relationship became the most talked about Tinseltown relationship of the Nineties. Pictures of them sunbathing nude together in the Caribbean only proved to heighten the public's rabid interest in their love life. For a couple that seemed so stable and solid, it came as shock to everyone when Pitt and Paltrow split up on 16 June 1997 – a mass of rumours hit the headlines at the time about why they had gone their separate ways but ultimately it would be Paltrow who would say later that she had been the architect of the relationship's demise.

Fast forward to the wedding day of Pitt and Aniston on 29 July 2000 and all those previous 'conquests' must have seemed somewhat irrelevant.

JENNIFER ANISTON

THE ONE WITH THE WEDDING

And now with several years of marriage under their belts – and despite scurrilous rumours in the press recently that Pitt and Aniston are ready to split up – it would seem that for a Hollywood marriage, the two's coupling is about as solid as a love born in Tinseltown can get. And according to the happy couple, it's only a matter of time before the world hears the pitt-er patter of small feet.

8

The one where *Friends* ends

JENNIFER ANISTON

THE ONE WHERE *FRIENDS* ENDS

Envied by millions all over the world, she had a hit show and a husband almost every woman on earth wanted to marry, as well as a movie career which, if not exactly soaring, was still bubbling away.

There were, however, a few new challenges for Jennifer to tackle. Including the ever-present paparazzi who still clamoured for pictures of Mr and Mrs Pitt. Clearly, Jennifer-mania was running higher than ever, and as a result, in a bizarre twist on an event which had previously befallen Brad, Jennifer found herself forced to sue after a particularly dedicated paparazzi photographed her topless.

JENNIFER ANISTON

THE ONE WHERE *FRIENDS* ENDS

So intent on photographing Jennifer had the snapper been that, in 1999, he had scaled an eight-foot wall and used a telephoto lens to snap shots of Jennifer sunbathing topless in her back garden. The resulting photographs graced the pages of US magazines *Celebrity Skin* and *High Society*, after circulating in France's *Voici*, Italy's *Eva Tremila* and, predictably, Britain's *Daily Sport* newspaper.

Proving she was no pushover, Jennifer brought suits against all the publications which printed the photographs as well as François Navarre, who she accused of invasion of privacy, trespassing and misappropriation of her name and likeness. Navarre successfully claimed that he wasn't the one who actually took the pictures, but did apologise to Jennifer for passing the pictures on to an agent based in Italy who sold them on for publication.

Navarre ended up paying substantial damages. A very clear warning was sent out to the rest of the world's paparazzi. This was not the first time a Pitt had sued over pictures. Previously Brad had sued *Playgirl* magazine for running full-frontal nude photos of him taken without his permission on a hotel balcony. The issue had been pulled from news stands, but not before it had become a collector's item.

These legal cases showed that while Jennifer and Brad were public figures, they weren't going to let their privacy be invaded. And anyway, the public were getting plenty of Jennifer on *Friends*, which was doing better than ever.

From smash-hit beginnings, *Friends* grew into a global phenomenon the likes of which hadn't been seen for years, as it played to huge audiences all over the world. It was eventually exported to China, where a thriving market in bootleg video copies had existed for ages. (The Chinese title translates as *Old Friends Stories!*)

As the show became bigger and bigger and bigger, Jennifer and the others graced more magazine covers, appeared as the subjects of more E! True Hollywood-style pop-documentaries, and seemed to be, literally, everywhere. Celebrities flocked to do guest appearances on the show, with the likes of Bruce Willlis, Chris Isaac, the Duchess of York, Sarah Ferguson and Jean-Claude Van Damme queuing up to appear. Freddie Prinze Jr. guested on the show's landmark 200th episode as a male nanny hired (briefly) by Ross and Rachel for their new baby, while Winona Ryder shared a

THE ONE WHERE *FRIENDS* ENDS

red-hot on-screen kiss with Rachel. Even the new Mr. Aniston, Brad Pitt himself, showed up as a former high-school friend of Ross who, ironically, couldn't stand Rachel. Meanwhile, Rachel's on-screen family was filled out with appearances by superstar Reece Witherspoon as one Green sister, Jill, and Christina Applegate as Rachel's other sibling, Amy. She also got a mother, portrayed by veteran actress Marlo Thomas. Thirty years earlier, Marlo had been in a Jennifer-like position herself as the star of a New York-set sitcom hit entitled *That Girl*. In a neat in-joke, one episode of *Friends* features Phoebe wearing a sweatshirt bearing a *That Girl* logo.

And as the show got bigger and bigger, it got longer too, as it went head-to-head with reality show hit *Survivor* by adding ten minutes to some episodes, and running forty minutes, unheard of for a sitcom, as it created "super-sized" *Friends*. It was, NBC boasted, "Must-See TV". And indeed it was, crowned as the defining sitcom of its generation, what *The Cosby Show* had been to the Eighties, *Friends* was to the Nineties.

It's widely thought that the series became such a hit as it captured a new phenomenon in life: while previous sitcoms had hinged on family or workplace settings, *Friends* was about a surrogate family formed by the friends, which is just what many of its 20-something viewers were doing, as they started working and living away from home.

And, like those 20-something viewers, and, of course, Jennifer herself, the show's characters grew with the series, mirroring the life changes of their real-life counterparts. Rachel and Ross got together and split up numerous times. Ross married British Emily, played by UK actress Helen Baxendale and star of *Cold Feet*, but their union didn't last long, largely due to the continuing presence of Rachel, giving Jennifer even more chances to showcase her finely honed comic talents. Having decided not to go to London for the wedding, Rachel changed her mind at the last minute and raced to be there. This caused further grief for Emily as Ross tripped over his vows, calling Emily "Rachel".

Even that didn't get Ross and Rachel back together, however, as they continued to play off each other and not-quite-manage to hook up. Still, at least Rachel had her new career in fashion to distract her (as well as a new haircut, after

JENNIFER ANISTON

THE ONE WHERE *FRIENDS* ENDS

Jennifer declared enough to be enough, and her character was allowed to lose "the Rachel" and adopt a longer, sleeker look.). First she was hired as a personal shopper, and then moved on to a job at top fashion house Ralph Lauren. Then she and Ross went to Vegas, got drunk, and the two woke up to find themselves married. Rachel pressed for an annulment, which Ross eventually got. In a later series, she and Ross got back together for one night, and Rachel fell pregnant with their daughter Emma. Eventually, the two wound up moving in together, platonically, after Emma's birth. All of which set the scene to get them back together as the end of the series finally loomed...

It had been almost 10 years since *Friends* started, an inordinately long time for any TV series to run, let alone for it to keep running successfully. On countless occasions, the question had been asked "How long can it keep going?" Not because the show was slipping in the ratings, it remained as high as ever, but because the cast wanted to move on to other things – there were always reports at contract re-negotiation time that at least one of them wasn't happy to continue because they wanted to do movies, and back at the beginning, they'd all promised that if one went, they all went. Plus

JENNIFER ANISTON

THE ONE WHERE *FRIENDS* ENDS

Jennifer, at least, was concerned that the show should not outstay its welcome along the lines of countless other series long past their sell-by-date when the final episode came. And she'd seemingly have been happy for it to go off the air at the end of its ninth season, saying when asked about returning the next autumn; "You've got six cast members and everybody has to be happy. I would have probably been okay with it ending then just because I felt like it. I want *Friends* to finish when people still like us."

The fact was that with nine years in the can, the *Friends* were expected to go off into the sunset. It's ninth-season premiere was the series most-watched episode ever, and, once again, was Rachel-centric, as it looked like Rachel might be going off into the arms of none other than Joey, while Ross was about to propose to her. In fact, several of the cast members were quoted as saying that yes, this really would be it.

But NBC had other ideas. *Friends*, insiders said, was unique, in that it seemed to be bullet-proof, riding high in the ratings and, more importantly, acting as a great launchpad for other new series, which could premiere in the slot immediately after it, guaranteeing that an awful lot of people would be watching when the new show started – and hopefully would become hooked on that too. Jennifer & co. were thus like gold dust and the girl who couldn't get a lead role at the High School for the Performing Arts was one of the most important players in the cut-throat multi-million dollar world of TV.

And the show was winning awards too, garnering an Emmy in 2002 for Outstanding Comedy Series, and another for Jennifer herself, as Outstanding Comedy Actress. Thus far, the show had been nominated for an amazing 44 Emmys and countless other awards (Lisa Kudrow had previously won one for the show too), and that made it even more of a golden goose.

While an advertising campaign urged fans to "cherish every episode" of season nine, behind the scenes, negotiations were going on to lure the stars back for season 10. Jennifer, it seemed was unlikely to commit to a full season of 24 episodes, and many thought that she would, perhaps, only be featured in a handful of the season's episodes, with high-profile guest stars "filling in" in the Rachel-free episodes. Ultimately, however, a compromise was agreed. All six would be back for season 10, but there would be just 18 episodes instead of the usual

THE ONE WHERE *FRIENDS* ENDS

24, with their salaries remaining the same at a cool $1 million an episode. NBC paid the producers an astounding $10 million an episode, however, a 40 per cent increase.

And season 10, subtitled "The Final Season" was on, padded out to full length by re-runs of "America's favourite episodes", as voted for in a phone-in-poll.

In spite of the reduced number of episodes, however, Jennifer and the others remained committed to making the show's last season a high-quality one, and Jennifer was quick to refute a news report that she had ordered producers to speed up the filming.

With news of the show's final demise came the questions, the speculation and the internet rumours – what would happen to the characters? Earlier, when it was thought that season nine would be the final season, a bizarre rumour had circulated, claiming that Rachel was to die in childbirth, leaving her baby to be raised by the newlywed Monica and Chandler. NBC quashed that one quickly, and set about keeping the actual final storylines under almost as tight security as had been featured at Brad and Jennifer's nuptials. In fact, had the season nine finale been the last episode ever, Rachel might have married Joey. Or Ross, which was what fans would clamour for her to do as the countdown to the *final* final show began.

The creators promised that the last ever season would see the *Friends* moving on with their lives. And indeed they did, as Phoebe married Mike (Jennifer's former movie co-star Paul Rudd), Monica and Chandler planned to adopt children and move to the suburbs, and Rachel was offered a job at Louis Vuitton in Paris, pushing Ross into a corner over his feelings for her.

Needless to say, the cast's feelings about the show ending were mixed. Even Jennifer, despite her fears it would go on too long, would be deeply saddened by the loss of something which had been so central to her life for such a long time, and which had given her much longed-for success.

"We're like very delicate china right now," she told reporters when asked about the casts' feelings regarding the impending finale. "And we're speeding toward a brick wall, inevitable pain... So that sounds fun, huh?" Helping them out were stars of smash-hits past, as reports had the six chatting with the likes of Mary Tyler

THE ONE WHERE *FRIENDS* ENDS

Moore (of *The Mary Tyler Moore Show*) and Danny DeVito (*Taxi*) to get tips on how to deal with gaining closure on a successful series.

Approximately five months before its scheduled airdate of Thursday, 6 May 2004, the cast gathered together to read through the script for the hour-long series finale – which they reacted positively to. The last show was taped a week or so later. Reportedly Jennifer burst into tears while filming a scene where James Michael Tyler's Gunther, long-time waiter at Central Perk who had an equally long-time crush on Rachel, finally declared his love for her.

And that was that. Except for the DVDs, the syndicated re-runs, the internet fan sites and all the other tie-ins which would ensure that Rachel Green and *Friends* live on forever. Matt LeBlanc's Joey, it was announced, would spinoff *Frasier*-style with his own show *Joey*, in which Joey moves to LA to seek stardom, and while Jennifer went down on record as saying she wouldn't mind guesting on his series, she nixed a reported *Friends* reunion special.

While reports claimed that the sextet had been offered $2 million each to do the reunion, Jennifer said she didn't want to cheapen the show and that the rumours were untrue. Reports also floated around that there would be a big-screen *Friends* movie, with rather more adult humour and possible nude scenes but little more was heard of that. One thing which Jennifer did tell reporters was that she and her co-stars would remain friends. Another element cited for the show's success was the way in which its six co-stars had bonded with each other immediately, giving audiences the sense that they really were friends with each other. She hoped, she said, that they would continue to see each other "The girls absolutely. The boys, we all love each other and I hope that we stay friends for a long time."

9

The one about
The Last One

JENNIFER ANISTON

THE ONE ABOUT THE LAST ONE

With *Friends* now officially over, here are a few facts about the very last episode...

• It was first broadcast in the US on 6 May 2004.

• Breaking with title tradition (all the other episodes are called *The One With...*) it was entitled *The Last One*.

• It was the 236th episode.

• 52.5 million US viewers watched it, more than the predicted 45 million.

JENNIFER ANISTON

THE ONE ABOUT THE LAST ONE

• 39.5 million watched the clip-show which was shown immediately before it.

• A 30-second commercial spot during the episode cost $2 million.

• Immediately after the show aired, the cast were interviewed on the Central Perk set by Jay Leno for his *Tonight Show*.

• In New York, the episode was shown on a big screen over Times Square.

• Under the auspices of the Tribeca Film Festival, some 3,000 people watched on another giant screen in a park overlooking the Hudson River.

• In the final scene, all the *Friends* turned in their keys to Monica's apartment – not that the door ever appeared to be locked...

• The episode was broadcast exactly one week before the series finale of another hit NBC sitcom, *Frasier*.

JENNIFER ANISTON

THE ONE ABOUT THE LAST ONE

And the *Friends* own personal endings:-

• Monica and Chandler adopted twins, gave up their apartment and moved to a suburban house.

• Phoebe and Mike stayed in New York, hinting that they would soon be starting a family of their own.

• Joey planned a move to Los Angeles to further his acting career – which will be the subject of next season's spin-off Joey. Amazingly, though, his impending move wasn't mentioned in *The Last One*.

• And of course Ross and Rachel... Rachel almost left NYC for a job in Paris, but was stopped at the airport by Ross, who had a mad cross-town dash to get there in time (complicated by Phoebe taking him to the wrong airport). He declared his love for Rachel one more time, but was rebuffed, only to return home sadly and find that Rachel had had a change of heart, run off the aeroplane and that she wanted to be with him too. Which was, of course, the ending everybody wanted.

10

The one with more successful movies

JENNIFER ANISTON

THE ONE WITH MORE SUCCESSFUL MOVIES

Way before *Friends* ended, Jennifer had been hard at work, still working away at her movie career, and she's been having a bit more success with it too.

Seemingly heeding the critics advice, and the realisation that of her movies thus far, the most successful had been *Object of My Affection*, she started to break away from the cookie-cutter romantic comedies that had received such a lukewarm reception, and attempted to banish the spectre of the Rachel-alike characters she had played in those films, and, indeed, the ghost of Rachel herself.

JENNIFER ANISTON

THE ONE WITH MORE SUCCESSFUL MOVIES

In 1998, while her romance with Brad Pitt was still in the future, Jennifer appeared in the little-seen but highly-acclaimed pseudo-documentary (about making a documentary), *The Thin Pink Line*, along with a whole load of other celebrities, including then-squeeze Tate Donovan, *Friends* co-star David Schwimmer, Mike Myers, Jason Priestly, Will Ferrell, Margaret Cho, Illeana Douglas and Janeane Garofalo. The few who saw it, loved it, and Jennifer's big screen street cred shot up almost immediately.

It went up even further the next year, when she became part of a bona fide cult classic, with the release of Mike Judge's working life satire *Office Space*.

Judge was also riding high thanks to television, having been the creator of the smash-hit MTV animated series *Beavis and Butt-Head*. *Office Space* was based on some of his other animation, and concerned a discontented office-worker named Peter (Ron Livingston), who hates his job and decides to plant a virus in the company's computer system which allows him and his friends to embezzle millions.

In truth, the embezzlement heist plot was little more than a contrivance to pad the script

THE ONE WITH MORE SUCCESSFUL MOVIES

out to the right length, as the film was mostly concerned with viciously satirising office life, with characters including a worker who had been laid off years ago, but hadn't realised as a computer glitch meant he was still receiving a salary, even though nobody ever gave him any work to do.

Jennifer starred as Joanna, a waitress at the diner/coffee house across the street, and who Peter is secretly in love with. While he railed against supervisors who endlessly reminded him that all reports needed cover sheets, she too had to deal with bureaucracy in the form of her manager, who insists that all employees wear a minimum of 15 badges/buttons/pins and that wearing just the minimum is indicative of not supporting the restaurant's spirit.

The George-Orwell-meets-*Saturday-Night-Live* outing wasn't a hit in cinemas, but good word-of-mouth on it swiftly spread, and it enjoyed massive popularity on video and DVD release (spawning collector and special edition DVDs). And even though Jennifer still hadn't had a box-office smash, *Office Space* did far more for her Hollywood career than any of her earlier rom-coms had, even though those had all gone into profit,

THE ONE WITH MORE SUCCESSFUL MOVIES

however marginal, while on first release.

Jennifer, it seemed, might actually be able to break out of the typecasting and prove that she is more than just the girl with great hair who can deliver a witty line while drinking coffee on TV.

Her next project proved even further how genuinely multi-talented she can be, as she didn't physically appear in it at all, but just gave her vocal skills to the character Annie Hughes, a single mother in 1958 small-town America, whose young son befriends a giant robot newly arrived from another planet, in the animated film *The Iron Giant*.

The film, based on a best-selling children's novel by Ted Hughes was hugely acclaimed and boasted plenty of vocal talent besides Jennifer. Vin Diesel voiced the robot itself, while Harry Connick Jr, Cloris Leachman, and Jennifer's *She's The One* co-star John Mahoney provided back-up. Critics adored its gentle story, as did many film buffs who appreciated the parallels between its Fifties setting and the actual America of the Fifties where alien robots often symbolically stood in for the much-feared communists of the era.

Yet again, however, it wasn't a smash hit, although it did prove once and for all that Jennifer had more than one string to her bow. Critics

singled out her vocal
plaudits, showing tha
on screen to garner
view, she could prob

Combining he
hectic *Friends* schedule was g
had to fit filming the movies in either while
show was on a break or by arranging shooting
around the sitcom's filming days on the weeks it
was being shot. But her tenacity had got her this
far, and she wasn't about to stop now.

Needless to say, there were disappointments
and missed parts along the way. She was forced to
drop out of an edgy comedy-drama called *The
Virgin Mary*, which would have seen her cast as a
virginal 29-year-old who finds herself falling for an
angst-ridden hit-man. The film was scheduled to
be shot while *Friends* wasn't filming but rewrites
on the script were so slow that by the time a final
draft came through, it was time for her to return to
shooting America's favourite sitcom.

But still she didn't let things get her down,
moving on and signing for a movie which looked like
it had all the ingredients of a summer smash hit.
Rock Star came in the wake of the hugely-popular
rock-music-themed *Almost Famous*. Like *Almost*

, it was also vaguely based in fact, its story
led on that of real-life rocker Tim "Ripper"
ens, part of a Judas Priest tribute band who
found himself called upon to become part of the real
thing when a space in the band opened up.

In the movie, rapper-turned-Calvin-Klein-
underwear-model-turned-actor Mark Wahlberg
plays Chris Cole, a part-time rocker who lives with
parents and scratches a living as a photocopier
repairman. But Chris lives for the evenings when
he gets to "be" his idol, Bobby Beers, frontman of
the fictional heavy metal legends Steel Dragon, in
a tribute band formed by Chris and his friends.
When one of Steel Dragon is kicked out of the band,
however, Cole – newly kicked out of his own tribute
group by his buddies - gets the phone call of a
lifetime, inviting him to join the real Steel Dragon.
Needless to say, he takes up the offer, only to find
that the reality is rather different from all his
dreams. Living his dream means he stands to lose
some things he'd never realised the importance of.

One of those things is his loving girlfriend
Emily, played by Jennifer, who believes in Chris
wholeheartedly, offering unconditional support,
only to find herself increasingly closed out from his
life as his fame grows.

JENNIFER ANISTON

THE ONE WITH MORE SUCCESSFUL MOVIES

The movie promised big things. Unfortunately, it didn't deliver them, disappointing critics and audiences alike. The box office take was minimal and the movie all but disappeared. Jennifer's role, which had looked so promising on paper, was, in fact, little more than a standard 'girlfriend' role.

But the disappointment of *Rock Star* was about to be completely obliterated from Jennifer's life, as she finally found a role millions of miles away from the likes of *Picture Perfect*'s Nina (and, for that matter, Rachel Green), and which would bring her acclaim, awards AND which would finally make the die-hard nay-sayers sit up and take notice of her.

The Good Girl was a comedy drama penned by Mike White and directed by Miguel Artega, a collaborative team who had previously produced the very-skewed and highly acclaimed *Chuck and Buck*.

Set in Texas, it starred Jennifer as Justine – a downtrodden, ill-educated white-trash cashier at a discount superstore. Justine was the sort of woman Rachel Green would probably have crossed the street to avoid (at least in her season one bratty phase) and not a single *Friend* would have been

THE ONE WITH MORE SUCCESSFUL MOVIES

caught dead shopping at Retail Rodeo, Justine's place of employment. Bored, depressed and 30-ish, Justine got no satisfaction out of anything, either her working life or her home life, as all she has to go home to is house-painter husband Phil (John C Reilly) who spends his days decorating homes with best bud Bubba (Tim Blake Nelson), and his evenings lounging on the couch (again with Bubba, who is, er, disturbingly close to Phil) and smoking pot.

So when a new cashier starts at the shop, and comes in the edgily sexy, 19-year-old form of indie actor Jake Gyllenhaal, it's no wonder Justine is fascinated by him. Especially when he informs her that his name is Holden, and sits around reading *The Catcher in the Rye*. Actually, his name is Tom, and he's a college dropout with a drinking problem, but he is still far more interesting than anything else going on in Justine's small Texas 'burb and very quickly he and Justine are enjoying a torrid affair.

Complications, however, ensue, when Bubba catches them at it, and demands sexual favours from Justine in return for not letting on to Phil. Further complications then ensue when Justine falls pregnant, and isn't sure who the father might be.

JENNIFER ANISTON

THE ONE WITH MORE SUCCESSFUL MOVIES

With its sex scenes, searing subject matter and indie sensibilities, *The Good Girl* was just what Jennifer's career needed. The critics loved the movie and they loved her.

Roger Ebert, one of America's most respected critics wrote in his *Chicago Sun-Times* review that "Jennifer Aniston has at last decisively broken with her '*Friends*' image in an independent film of satiric fire and emotional turmoil. It will no longer be possible to consider her in the same way."

Indeed making the film had been a challenge for Jennifer. as she'd had to really push herself to get into Justine's character and completely obliterate all traces of the bouncy Rachel. "I had to lose all the smiles and hand gestures I do as Rachel for the part of Justine because she's so miserable," she told reporters. "My acting coach had me sitting on my hands. I also had to walk around with three pound weights strapped to my wrists and ankles to develop her slumping posture and her shuffling loser gait." The hard work paid off however, as Jennifer received her first award nomination for something besides straight comedy, being nominated for an Independent Spirit Award for her work as Justine.

And with *The Good Girl* safely in the bag,

JENNIFER ANISTON

THE ONE WITH MORE SUCCESSFUL MOVIES

Jennifer really was up and running. By the time news was reaching fans around the world that *Friends* really was on its way out, she was up on the big screen again, this time back in a commercial property, but one which would fulfil all its box office promise. And while the role was again, that of the hero's love interest, this time the hero was at least a genuine A-list superstar.

Jim Carrey headlined *Bruce Almighty* as a small-town TV newsman who misses out on promotion and blames his failure on God (Morgan Freeman). Taking exception to this, God grants Carrey's character omnipotence, turning all deity duties over to the rubber-faced funnyman, who then finds that being the all-powerful ruler of the earth isn't as easy as it looks. Jennifer plays his fiancée, kindergarten teacher Grace, who he almost loses, but then – in true Hollywood fashion – gets back at the end, just in the nick of time.

While her part sounded similar to that of Emily in *Rock Star*, this time the script was first-rate, and *Bruce Almighty* took over $200 million in the US alone. Granted, there were a few hair-raising moments on-set, including one dramatic moment when Carrey actually saved her from what could potentially have been a life-threatening

THE ONE WITH MORE SUCCESSFUL MOVIES

situation, when high winds caused a crane on set to topple over, and he swiftly pushed Jennifer out of its path. But while Jennifer was mightily grateful to the comedy star for saving her from being squashed, Carrey also did do his share of damage, Jennifer later told reporters, as their bedroom scene was highly energetic. "He just grabbed me, lifted me up and threw me on to the bed. It was like a wrestling throw. I've never been so bruised in my life as I have been working with Jim Carrey. I was black and blue," she said, talking about the experience of working with Carrey which she nonetheless insisted she had enjoyed.

With a critically acclaimed dramatic performance and a smash hit comedy under her belt, Jennifer was now starting to establish herself firmly as a lady to be reckoned with. She also seemed to be something of a glutton for punishment, or certainly a workaholic as at one point, she was filming on *Friends*, *Bruce Almighty* and her next hit, *Along Came Polly*, all at once.

Polly, which hit theatres a few months before *Friends* bowed out, was another number one box office smash, in spite of rather cool reviews, and gave Jennifer far more than just another girlfriend role, opposite another comedy star, Ben Stiller

THE ONE WITH MORE SUCCESSFUL MOVIES

(proving how incestuous the A-list really is, Stiller had previously directed Jim Carrey in the comedy *The Cable Guy*). She starred as the free-spirited Polly, owner of a blind pet ferret(!) with whom Stiller, as an ultra-cautious risk analyst begins an affair, cheating on his new wife, another sitcom redhead, *Will & Grace*'s Debra Messing. While the reviews were, indeed, not nearly as top-flight as most had been for *Bruce Almighty*, they still cited Jennifer as one of the main reasons to see the film, with her zany performance standing out against the rather contrived plot. She held her own with big-screen veteran Stiller as well, just as she had with Carrey, with reviewer James Berardinelli claiming "Aniston is as adept at comedy as Stiller".

Originally entitled *Risk*, *Along Came Polly* proved one thing for sure: that Jennifer Aniston wasn't a box office risk when it came to casting female leads – it grossed $32 million in its US opening weekend alone. And three months later had taken double the $42 million it had cost to make. *Friends* might be on its way out, but as Jennifer bade farewell to the show which had made her a star.she did so with the husband, the career and the life she'd always longed for,

11

The one with the future

JENNIFER ANISTON

THE ONE WITH THE FUTURE

She has been part of what is arguably the most successful TV series in history. She has been been critically acclaimed for her movie performances. She has married to one of the most desirable men in the world. Surely she can't have found time to accomplish anything else...?

Well, there is the impressive list of award nominations and victories, without mention of which no chronicle of Jennifer's life would be complete. From the sublime to the ridiculous, she's been nominated for four Emmies, as Outstanding Supporting Actress in a Comedy Series in 2000 and 2001. The six *Friends* initially agreed that

THE ONE WITH THE FUTURE

they were all "supporting" artistes and would not compete in the "lead" categories, but then changed their minds, and Jennifer ran in the Lead Comedy/Musical actress categories for 2002 and 2003, winning in 2002. She's also got no less than three Funniest Supporting Female Performer in a TV Series American Comedy nominations, from 1996, 1999 and 2001, and a Golden Globe from 2003, as well as a nomination for another from 2002. Four years running – 2001, 2002, 2003 and 2004, she's taken home the Best Foreign TV Personality Aftonbladet TV Prize from Sweden, and was 2002 Actress of the Year at the Hollywood Film Festival. *The Good Girl* got her a 2003 Best Female Lead nomination at the Independent Spirit Awards, and another from the Online Film Critics Society. It also got her a nomination at the 2003 Golden Satellite Awards for Best Performance by an Actress in a Comedy or Musical Film. In fact she had two reasons to attend that ceremony, as she was also nominated for Best Performance by an Actress in a TV Musical/Comedy for *Friends* – she'd also had that nomination in 2000.

She was the prestigious People's Choice Awards Winner for Favourite Female Television

JENNIFER ANISTON

THE ONE WITH THE FUTURE

Performer in 2001, 2002, 2003 and 2004, and has multiple nominations from the Screen Actors Guild: as part of the *Friends* ensemble in 1999, 2000, 2001, 2002, 2003 and 2004, with nominations as Outstanding Performance by a Female Actor in a Comedy in 2002 and 2003. The *Friends* sextet also shared a 2000 *TV Guide* Award for Editors Choice – and there was also, er, a 1997 Razzie Award "Worst Newcomer" nomination shared by Jennifer, Matt Le Blanc, David Schwimmer and Lisa Kudrow as the *Friends* stars became movie-wannabes.

She's had best overall hair and highlights in a Wella celebrity hair survey conducted in 2003, topped the 2003 Forbes Top 100 Celebrity list, deposing the 2002 winner Britney Spears by earning $35 million in 2002 and appearing on more magazine covers than any rival celeb. Previously, she'd also been named Entertainer of the year by the E! Entertainment TV network for her work on *Friends* and *The Good Girl*.

Oh, and just to balance out all the acting/achievement awards with something a bit more shallow, she also ranked in *FHM*'s 100 Sexiest Women as number six in 1996, number two in 1997, number four in 1998, number six

THE ONE WITH THE FUTURE

again in 1999, number 10 in 2000 and number 55 in 2001. She was also at number 11 in *Celebrity Sleuth's* 25 Sexiest Women of 1997 and number nine in *E!'s* 2002 Sexiest Women Entertainers. Not bad, huh?

Besides that, she's also managed to be something of a life-saver on no less than two occasions – in August 2002, she performed the Heimlich manoeuvre on a choking diner at a Mexican restaurant in Hollywood. While dining on her favourite tacos and burritos, Jennifer heard the man choking on a nacho, and used the life-saving skills she'd learned years previously to save the man's life. And that came just a month or so after a workman carrying out building work on Brad and Jennifer's home had fired a nail through his hand with a nail-gun. Jennifer turned nurse, removing the offending object, and using towels and a first aid kit on the unfortunate builder, ensuring that no bones or tendons had been damaged.

Jennifer had also shown her compassionate side earlier when she was the only Hollywood celebrity to visit the incarcerated actor Robert Downey Jr. in May 2000. Downey, who was serving a three-year-sentence for a probation violation, was

THE ONE WITH THE FUTURE

depressed and had been attacked by fellow inmates at California's notoriously tough Corcoran Jail. Downey's former agent Jerry Goldstein told press that out of several Hollywood stars who had been asked to visit the actor, only Jennifer showed up – in spite of her anti-drugs stance.

"Jennifer was there for me when other so-called friends turned their backs. Thanks to her, I have hope, a way out... Before there was none. I'd even thought of doing myself a favour by ending it all," Downey told Goldstein.

She's also showed the same tolerance in her relationship with Pitt, making it clear that in a town where marriages come and go and are often based on business more than love, theirs is a true union. She even went along with her hunky husband to a Buddhist Monastery, even though, at least to other attendees, she didn't seem to be quite as passionate about the Eastern religion herself.

"She listened to everything anyone said, but in that too-eager way people do when they're just doing it to please others. She thought his painting was cute and clearly adores Brad - they couldn't keep their hands off each other," a fellow attendee told reporters.

Indeed, it seems to many that Jennifer's next

THE ONE WITH THE FUTURE

big production might not be a movie or a TV series at all. Reportedly, Brad and Jennifer are both very keen on having children as soon as possible, having started building a nanny's quarters and a playroom on to their home as far back as 2002, with Jennifer telling press, "We definitely want to have kids. I always thought of two or three children, but Brad wants seven. He loves the idea of a huge family."

She was later widely quoted as saying that she still wants "an Oscar and a baby" and indeed, at one point, reports hinted that she might even end her acting career in order to start a family. In fact her and Brad wanting children is widely thought to have been one of the biggest sticking points over whether or not she'd sign for *Friends* season 10, with sources quoting her at the time as saying "In my mind I'm done. I want to start my family."

In fact the only time reports have appeared in the press suggesting that the state of affairs at Casa Pitt may be anything other than blissful have been when they've concerned the duo's plans for a family – and all have been as strenuously denied as any reports of an actual pregnancy. One report had the duo "in negotiations" over having a baby, and others having Jennifer demanding the

THE ONE WITH THE FUTURE

speeding-up of shooting on *Friends* series 10 as Brad was unhappy that she'd even committed to making it. Swiftly rubbished by Aniston's camp.

The duo's relationship is strong – not to mention sizzling along nicely, as Hollywood rumour placed the couple squarely in the bedroom for the whole of Christmas 2002, showering each other with X-rated gifts including sexy underwear, XXX-rated movies and massage oil. Jennifer also went wild for a 2002 Hollywood exercise craze which saw dozens of Hollywood ladies signing up for Cardio Striptease classes at LA's trendy Crunch gym, where the likes of Jennifer, Carmen Electra and Angelica Bridges stripped along to music while doing some wild moves to keep off the pounds. Needless to say, they didn't go all the way, but former *Baywatch*-babe Bridges said, "I thought they would be using poles and straddling chairs, and doing all this crazy stuff, but it's actually the best workout I've ever had."

One newspaper, however, had a source claiming that as well as using the workouts to keep her weight down, she was also using them as a source of entertainment for Brad by putting on private shows at home.

All of which may well mean the baby plans

THE ONE WITH THE FUTURE

coming together pretty soon, as 2004 saw the duo inviting friends with kids over to critique their house on how baby-friendly it is. Gossip in the three female star's luxury dressing rooms was also baby-centric as *Friends* came to an end, according to sources on the show, who said that kids were all the girls talked about: "Fertility tips, pregnancy tips, baby fashion - you name it! It's been so much fun watching Jen, Courteney and Lisa talking about kids and parenting. Ten years ago they were all cooing over who they had a crush on - things have definitely changed."

Reports have also painted a picture of Jennifer as being keen to patch things up with her own mother Nancy. Speaking in an interview, Jennifer said "I think there comes a point where you have to grow up and get over yourself and forgive. I definitely see that there's hope. I see myself, I look in the mirror...and I'm like, 'Oh my God, you're Nancy. You've become her, so you may as well call her.'"

The Pitts are also making sure that they get plenty of opportunity to work together as well, having started their own production company, Plan B, with producers Brad Grey and Michael Siegel. The company signed a deal with Warner Brothers

THE ONE WITH THE FUTURE

to produce movies, and Brad and Jennifer were said to be hoping to do a remake of the classic *Charlie and the Chocolate Factory*, as well as optioning various other scripts. The jury is still out, however, on whether they two will appear together in front of the camera, or just stick to producing together, with one source claiming that as Brad previously dated and split with two of his leading ladies (Juliette Lewis and Gwyneth Paltrow), he treasures his marriage to Jennifer too much to risk the possibility of history repeating itself. "They call couples working together the kiss of death – and I might be an example!" he told reporters.

Whatever the case, Jennifer will be on our screens again soon, with a remake of Sixties thriller *Gambit* up next for her, plus two other as yet untitled projects.

She's also become politically active, having worked alongside other stars including Leonardo DiCaprio, Barbra Streisand, Meg Ryan and Kevin Costner to raise funds for Democratic Presidential Candidate John Kerry, joining a fund raiser in April 2004 which included a mini concert by James Taylor and stand-up comedy from Maestro Larry David, creator of *Seinfeld* and *Curb Your Enthusiasm*.

JENNIFER ANISTON

THE ONE WITH THE FUTURE

She and Brad previously were patrons of a project launched by one of David's *Seinfeld* buddies, Jason Alexander, who became the public face of the One Voice campaign, seeking opinions from Israelis and Palestinians themselves on how to resolve their long-running conflict. Brad and Jennifer attended the project's launch and are big supporters of it.

But in the face of her massive fame, wealth and success, what keeps Jennifer so appealing to her fans is her overwhelming normality and sense of humour. Unlike so many Hollywood divas, she's kept her feet on the ground, humourously telling everyone in 2001 that the secret to her shiny hair was a horse shampoo called Mane and Tail, and then that she actually couldn't believe she'd married THE Brad Pitt of Hollywood super-fame until she went to the dentist to have her wisdom teeth removed and the nurse came out and called for Mrs Pitt. (she changed her name to Pitt 18 months after the couple wed.)

And so Jennifer's achieved all that she ever dreamed of – the fame, the success, and most of all, being happy in herself, her success banishing the self doubt she'd fought so hard to overcome in her teens. She even finally got to meet Simon LeBon,

THE ONE WITH THE FUTURE

bumping into him in Santa Barbara one day.

"Brad and I ran into Simon Le Bon a couple of months ago." She told journalists. "I'm looking at something and I see Brad going, 'Dude! You gotta come here.' And I walk over and Simon was literally standing right there. I was like, 'Oh, my God.' Then I went up to him and said, 'I waited outside a hotel for you.' I think he thought we were nuts."

Whether he did or not, millions worldwide – and they include one of the world's most famous leading men – think she's *Picture Perfect*.

12

The one with old Friends

JENNIFER ANISTON

THE ONE WITH OLD FRIENDS

Friends may have made Jennifer into a household name, but she couldn't have done it without her other *Friends* – all five of them. So here's the lowdown on the other five members of the cast and their characters:

Courteney Cox-Arquette/Monica Geller

Courteney Cox was born into a wealthy family in Alabama. She dropped out of an architecture course to pursue modelling and was signed by the prestigious Ford Agency. She appeared in numerous teen magazines and in TV adverts. Making her acting debut on the soap opera *As the World Turns*, she got

JENNIFER ANISTON

THE ONE WITH OLD FRIENDS

her big break when she was cast by Brian DePalma in Bruce Springsteen's *Dancing in the Dark* video. Moving to LA, she won the part of Michael J Fox's girlfriend on the hit sitcom *Family Ties*, before appearing in numerous films and landing the role of Monica. She has since appeared in the super-successful *Scream* horror franchise, and married actor David Arquette in 1999.

Formerly fat, Monica Geller is a chef who loves to cook and to make sure that all things are kept in order at all times. Having lived rather in the shadow of her older brother Ross, and pretty friend Rachel, she emerged as a strong character who was the unofficial leader of the group. After taking in runaway bride Rachel, and helping Ross through his divorce, Monica dealt with losing her job at trendy NYC restaurant Iridium and being forced to work at a 1950's style diner – in fifties costume – before getting back on her feet. She dated older man Richard (Tom Selleck) before finding love with former platonic friend Chandler, who she married and eventually adopted twin babies with.

JENNIFER ANISTON

THE ONE WITH OLD FRIENDS

Lisa Kudrow/Phoebe Buffay

Born in Encino, California, Lisa Kudrow is considerably more intellectual than her ditzy onscreen character, having graduated from the prestigious Vassar College in New York with a BA in Biology. Originally intent on a career in medical research, she moved to LA where she was inspired to take up comedy and worked in improve theatre. Cast as waitress Ursula on sitcom *Mad About You*, she then won the role of Phoebe – who became Ursula's twin sister. Lisa has also starred in the hit movies *Romy and Michelle's High School Reunion* and *Analyze This*. Married to advertising executive Michael Stern, she has one son, Julian.

Phoebe Buffay hasn't had the easiest life – her father ran off and left her early on in life, then her mother committed suicide, leaving her to be raised by her cab-driving grandmother. Nevertheless Phoebe put a brave face on things, dealing with her evil twin Ursula and everything else life threw at her with a loopy sense of humour. Following her grandmother's death, she tracked down her father and brother, then played surrogate mother to her brother's children. After an affair with a research scientist and others, she finally met and married Mike, and looks set to live happily ever after.

THE ONE WITH OLD FRIENDS

Matt LeBlanc/Joey Tribbiani

Born in Massachusetts, Matt LeBlanc isn't as Italian as his onscreen alter-ego Joey – although he does have some Italian in him. Along with a little French, Irish, Dutch and English. Having worked as a model, he appeared in numerous commercials, including spots for Levis and Coca-Cola, before breaking into film and landing the part of Joey in Friends. He is married to model Melissa McKnight and the two have one daughter, Marina.

Good-hearted actor Joey Tribbiani is great at getting girls, giving advice about girls to his neurotic roommate Chandler and eating. Not so good at acting, though. In fact most of his early parts ended in failure, including his stint in avant-garde musical *Freud!* being a body double and appearing on a VD-warning poster. Eventually Joey did get a break, however, being cast as Dr. Drake Ramore on the soap opera *Days of Our Lives*, only to lose it again after claiming in an interview that he wrote his own lines. Eventually rehired, he had many liaisons with many ladies, but never found that special someone...

JENNIFER ANISTON

THE ONE WITH OLD FRIENDS

Matthew Perry/Chandler Bing

Born in the US but brought up in Canada, Matthew Perry became a high-ranked junior tennis player before moving to LA to live with his actor father. He began his acting career straight out of school, appearing in the TV series *Second Chance*, and went on to make many other film and TV appearances, including one alongside River Phoenix in *A Night in the Life of Jimmy Reardon*, before being cast as Chandler Bing. His films since *Friends* include *The Whole Nine Yards*, *Three To Tango* and *Fools Rush In*. A former beau of Julia Roberts, Matthew is still single.

Super-sarcastic and always ready with a one-liner put-down, Chandler Bing was Ross' college roommate, and worked as a data processor at a nameless faceless conglomerate. Often mistaken as gay (much to his consternation), Chandler didn't have much luck with the ladies (serial-dating the ultra-whiny Janice), or with the parents, as his mother was a flamboyant writer and his father a transvestite. He did, however, get trapped in an ATM vestibule with a supermodel and then fell for his best friend's sister, first living with and then marrying Monica.

THE ONE WITH OLD FRIENDS

David Schwimmer/Ross Geller

Born in Los Angeles, David Schwimmer attended Beverly Hills High School (of *Beverly Hills 90210* fame) before attending Northwestern University where he studied speech and theatre. After founding Chicago's Looking Glass Theatre Company, he returned to LA and appeared in the hit series *The Wonder Years*, along with various other roles before being cast as Ross. He dated singer Natalie Imbruglia and Israeli actress Mili Avital, but is still unmarried. Since making *Friends*, David has appeared in several films including *Kissing a Fool* and *The Pallbearer* as well as the highly-acclaimed mini series *Band of Brothers*.

Neurotic but lovable paleontologist Ross Geller was always his parents' favourite. Not that that did him much good when his wife turned out to be a lesbian and left him for another woman. Nor did it help him with his life-long crush on sister Monica's high-school friend Rachel. In fact after Rachel came back into their lives, it took Ross an entire season to get the message across that he liked her. The two then embarked on an on-again, off-again relationship which would last ten years and survive Ross' disastrous marriage to British Emily, an accidental marriage between them in

JENNIFER ANISTON

THE ONE WITH OLD FRIENDS

Las Vegas, and the equally accidental conception of baby Emma. Needless to say, when the final curtain came down, though, the two were together.

13

Filmography

JENNIFER ANISTON

FILMOGRAPHY

Camp Cucamonga (1990)
(AKA How I Spent My Summer)
Ava Schector
Molloy (TV, 1990)
Courtney
Ferris Bueller (TV, 1990)
Jeannie Bueller
The Edge (TV, 1992)
Various
Leprechaun (1993)
Tory Reding
Muddling Through (TV, 1994)
Madeline Drego Cooper
Friends (TV, 1994-2004)
Rachel Green
Dream for an Insomniac (1996)
Allison
She's The One (1996)
Renee Fitzpatrick
Picture Perfect (1997)
Kate Mosely
Til There Was You (1997)
Debbie
The Object of My Affection (1998)
Nina Borowski

JENNIFER ANISTON

The Thin Pink Line (1998)
Clove
Office Space (1999)
Joanna
The Iron Giant (1999)
Annie Hughes (Voice)
Rock Star (2001)
Emily Poule
The Good Girl (2002)
Justine Last
Bruce Almighty (2003)
Grace Connelly
Along Came Polly (2004)
Polly Prince
Gambit (2006)

DID YOU KNOW ABOUT FRIENDS?

What is Chandler and Joey's favourite TV show?

Answer: *Baywatch*

What does Joey do when he is reading a really scary book?

Answer: He puts the book in the freezer

JENNIFER ANISTON

DID YOU KNOW ABOUT FRIENDS?

What is Monica's parents' nickname for her?

Answer: Harmonica

What is Chandler's nubbin?

Answer: A third nipple

Which 'Friend' hasn't slept with Janice?

Answer: Joey

BIOGRAPHIES

OTHER BOOKS IN THE SERIES

Also available in the series:

OTHER BOOKS IN THE SERIES

DAVID BECKHAM

This book covers the amazing life of the boy from East London who has not only become a world class footballer and the captain of England, but also an idol to millions, and probably the most famous man in Britain.

His biography tracks his journey, from the playing fields of Chingford to the Bernabau. It examines how he joined his beloved Manchester United and became part of a golden generation of talent that led to United winning trophies galore.

Beckham's parallel personal life is also examined, as he moved from tongue-tied football-obsessed kid to suitor of a Spice Girl, to one half of Posh & Becks, the most famous celebrity couple in Britain – perhaps the world. His non-footballing activities, his personal indulgences and changing styles have invited criticism, and even abuse, but his football talent has confounded the critics, again and again.

The biography looks at his rise to fame and his relationship with Posh, as well as his decision to leave Manchester for Madrid. Has it affected his relationship with Posh? What will the latest controversy over his sex life mean for celebrity's royal couple? And will he come back to play in England again?

OTHER BOOKS IN THE SERIES

GEORGE CLOONEY

The tale of George Clooney's astonishing career is an epic every bit as riveting as one of his blockbuster movies. It's a story of tenacity and determination, of fame and infamy, a story of succeeding on your own terms regardless of the risks. It's also a story of emergency rooms, batsuits, tidal waves and killer tomatoes, but let's not get ahead of ourselves.

Born into a family that, by Sixties' Kentucky standards, was dripping with show business glamour, George grew up seeing the hard work and heartache that accompanied a life in the media spotlight.

By the time stardom came knocking for George Clooney, it found a level-headed and mature actor ready and willing to embrace the limelight, while still indulging a lifelong love of partying and practical jokes. A staunchly loyal friend and son, a bachelor with a taste for the high life, a vocal activist for the things he believes and a born and bred gentleman; through failed sitcoms and blockbuster disasters, through artistic credibility and box office success, George Clooney has remained all of these things...and much, much more. Prepare to meet Hollywood's most fascinating megastar in this riveting biography.

OTHER BOOKS IN THE SERIES

BILLY CONNOLLY

In a 2003 London Comedy Poll to find Britain's favourite comedian, Billy Connolly came out on top. It's more than just Billy Connolly's all-round comic genius that puts him head and shoulders above the rest. Connolly has also proved himself to be an accomplished actor with dozens of small and big screen roles to his name. In 2003, he could be seen in *The Last Samurai* with Tom Cruise.

Connolly has also cut the mustard in the USA, 'breaking' that market in a way that chart-topping pop groups since The Beatles and the Stones have invariably failed to do, let alone mere stand-up comedians. Of course, like The Beatles and the Stones, Billy Connolly has been to the top of the pop charts too with D.I.V.O.R.C.E. in 1975.

On the way he's experienced heartache of his own with a difficult childhood and a divorce of his own, found the time and energy to bring up five children, been hounded by the press on more than one occasion, and faced up to some considerable inner demons. But Billy Connolly is a survivor. Now in his 60s, he's been in show business for all of 40 years, and 2004 finds him still touring. This exciting biography tells the story an extraordinary entertainer.

OTHER BOOKS IN THE SERIES

ROBERT DE NIRO

Robert De Niro is cinema's greatest chameleon. Snarling one minute, smirking the next, he's straddled Hollywood for a quarter of a century, making his name as a serious character actor, in roles ranging from psychotic taxi drivers to hardened mobsters. The scowls and pent-up violence may have won De Niro early acclaim but, ingeniously, he's now playing them for laughs, poking fun at the tough guy image he so carefully cultivated. Ever the perfectionist, De Niro holds nothing back on screen, but in real life he is a very private man – he thinks of himself as just another guy doing a job. Some job, some guy. There's more to the man than just movies. De Niro helped New York pick itself up after the September 11 terrorist attacks on the Twin Towers by launching the TriBeCa Film Festival and inviting everyone downtown. He runs several top-class restaurants and has dated some of the most beautiful women in the world, least of all supermodel Naomi Campbell. Now in his 60s, showered with awards and a living legend, De Niro's still got his foot on the pedal. There are six, yes six, films coming your way in 2004. In this latest biography, you'll discover all about his latest roles and the life of this extraordinary man.

OTHER BOOKS IN THE SERIES

MICHAEL DOUGLAS

Douglas may have been a shaggy-haired member of a hippy commune in the Sixties but just like all the best laidback, free-loving beatniks, he's gone on to blaze a formidable career, in both acting and producing.

In a career that has spanned nearly 40 years so far, Douglas has produced a multitude of hit movies including the classic *One Flew Over The Cuckoo's Nest* and *The China Syndrome* through to box office smashes such as *Starman* and *Face/Off*.

His acting career has been equally successful – from *Romancing The Stone* to *Wall Street* to *Fatal Attraction*, Douglas's roles have shown that he isn't afraid of putting himself on the line when up there on the big screen.

His relationship with his father; his stay in a top clinic to combat his drinking problem; the breakdown of his first marriage; and his publicised clash with the British media have all compounded to create the image of a man who's transformed himself from being the son of Hollywood legend Kirk Douglas, into Kirk Douglas being the dad of Hollywood legend, Michael Douglas.

OTHER BOOKS IN THE SERIES

HUGH GRANT

He's the Oxford fellow who stumbled into acting, the middle-class son of a carpet salesman who became famous for bumbling around stately homes and posh weddings. The megastar actor who claims he doesn't like acting, but has appeared in over 40 movies and TV shows.

On screen he's romanced a glittering array of Hollywood's hottest actresses, and tackled medical conspiracies and the mafia. Off screen he's hogged the headlines with his high profile girlfriend as well as finding lifelong notoriety after a little Divine intervention in Los Angeles.

Hugh Grant is Britain's biggest movie star, an actor whose talent for comedy has often been misjudged by those who assume he simply plays himself.

From bit parts in Nottingham theatre, through comedy revues at the Edinburgh Fringe, and on to the top of the box office charts, Hugh has remained constant – charming, witty and ever so slightly sarcastic, obsessed with perfection and performance while winking to his audience as if to say: "This is all awfully silly, isn't it?" Don't miss this riveting biography.

OTHER BOOKS IN THE SERIES

MICHAEL JACKSON

Friday 29 August 1958 was not a special day in Gary, Indiana, and indeed Gary, was far from being a special place. But it was on this day and in this location that the world's greatest entertainer was to be born, Michael Joseph Jackson.

The impact that this boy was destined to have on the world of entertainment could never have been estimated. Here we celebrate Michael Jackson's extraordinary talents, and plot the defining events over his 40-year career. This biography explores the man behind the myth, and gives an understanding of what drives this special entertainer.

In 1993, there was an event that was to rock Jackson's world. His friendship with a 12-year-old boy and the subsequent allegations resulted in a lawsuit, a fall in record sales and a long road to recovery. Two marriages, three children and 10 years later there is a feeling of déjà vu as Jackson again deals with more controversy. Without doubt, 2004 proves to be the most important year in the singer's life. Whatever that future holds for Jackson, his past is secured, there has never been and there will never again be anything quite like Michael Jackson.

OTHER BOOKS IN THE SERIES

NICOLE KIDMAN

On 23 March 2003 Nicole Kidman won the Oscar for Best Actress for her role as Virginia Woolf in *The Hours.* That was the night that marked Nicole Kidman's acceptance into the upper echelons of Hollywood royalty. She had certainly come a long way from the 'girlfriend' roles she played when she first arrived in Hollywood – in films such as *Billy Bathgate* and *Batman Forever* – although even then she managed to inject her 'pretty girl' roles with an edge that made her acting stand out. And she was never merely content to be Mrs Cruise, movie star's wife. Although she stood dutifully behind her then husband in 1993 when he was given his star on the Hollywood Walk of Fame, Nicole got a star of her own 10 years later, in 2003.

Not only does Nicole Kidman have stunning good looks and great pulling power at the box office, she also has artistic credibility. But Nicole has earned the respect of her colleagues, working hard and turning in moving performances from a very early age. Although she dropped out of school at 16, no one doubts the intelligence and passion that are behind the fiery redhead's acting career, which includes television and stage work, as well as films. Find out how Kidman became one of Hollywood's most respected actresses in this compelling biography.

OTHER BOOKS IN THE SERIES

JENNIFER LOPEZ

There was no suggestion that the Jennifer Lopez of the early Nineties would become the accomplished actress, singer and icon that she is today. Back then she was a dancer on the popular comedy show *In Living Color* – one of the Fly Girls, the accompaniment, not the main event. In the early days she truly was Jenny from the block; the Bronx native of Puerto Rican descent – another hopeful from the east coast pursuing her dreams in the west.

Today, with two marriages under her belt, three multi-platinum selling albums behind her and an Oscar-winning hunk as one of her ex-boyfriends, she is one of the most talked about celebrities of the day. Jennifer Lopez is one of the most celebrated Hispanic actresses of all time.

Her beauty, body and famous behind, are lusted after by men and envied by women throughout the world. She has proven that she can sing, dance and act. Yet her critics dismiss her as a diva without talent. And the criticisms are not just about her work, some of them are personal. But what is the reality? Who is Jennifer Lopez, where did she come from and how did get to where she is now? This biography aims to separate fact from fiction to reveal the real Jennifer Lopez.

OTHER BOOKS IN THE SERIES

MADONNA

Everyone thought they had Madonna figured out in early 2003. The former Material Girl had become Maternal Girl, giving up on causing controversy to look after her two children and set up home in England with husband Guy Ritchie. The former wild child had settled down and become respectable. The new Madonna would not do anything to shock the establishment anymore, she'd never do something like snogging both Britney Spears and Christina Aguilera at the MTV Video Music Awards... or would she?

Of course she would. Madonna has been constantly reinventing herself since she was a child, and her ability to shock even those who think they know better is both a tribute to her business skills and the reason behind her staying power. Only Madonna could create gossip with two of the current crop of pop princesses in August and then launch a children's book in September. In fact, only Madonna would even try.

In her 20-year career she has not just been a successful pop singer, she is also a movie star, a business woman, a stage actress, an author and a mother. Find out all about this extraordinary modern-day icon in this new compelling biography.

OTHER BOOKS IN THE SERIES

BRAD PITT

From the launch pad that was his scene stealing turn in *Thelma And Louise* as the sexual-enlightening bad boy. To his character-driven performances in dramas such as *Legends of the Fall* through to his Oscar-nominated work in *Twelve Monkeys* and the dark and razor-edged Tyler Durden in *Fight Club*, Pitt has never rested on his laurels. Or his good looks.

And the fact that his love life has garnered headlines all over the world hasn't hindered Brad Pitt's profile away from the screen either – linked by the press to many women, his relationships with the likes of Juliette Lewis and Gwyneth Paltrow. Then of course, in 2000, we had the Hollywood fairytale ending when he tied the silk knot with Jennifer Aniston.

Pitt's impressive track record as a superstar, sex symbol *and* credible actor looks set to continue as he has three films lined up for release over the next year – as Achilles in the Wolfgang Peterson-helmed Troy; Rusty Ryan in the sequel *Ocean's Twelve* and the titular Mr Smith in the thriller *Mr & Mrs Smith* alongside Angelina Jolie. Pitt's ever-growing success shows no signs of abating. Discover all about Pitt's meteoric rise from rags to riches in this riveting biography.

OTHER BOOKS IN THE SERIES

SHANE RICHIE

Few would begrudge the current success of 40-year-old Shane Richie. To get where he is today, Shane has had a rather bumpy roller coaster ride that has seen the hard working son of poor Irish immigrants endure more than his fair share of highs and lows – financially, professionally and personally.

In the space of four decades he has amused audiences at school plays, realised his childhood dream of becoming a Pontins holiday camp entertainer, experienced homelessness, beat his battle with drink, became a million-aire then lost the lot. He's worked hard and played hard.

When the producers of *EastEnders* auditioned Shane for a role in the top TV soap, they decided not to give him the part, but to create a new character especially for him. That character was Alfie Moon, manager of the Queen Vic pub, and very quickly Shane's TV alter ego has become one of the most popular soap characters in Britain. This biography is the story of a boy who had big dreams and never gave up on turning those dreams into reality

OTHER BOOKS IN THE SERIES

JONNY WILKINSON

"There's 35 seconds to go, this is the one. It's coming back for Jonny Wilkinson. He drops for World Cup glory. It's over! He's done it! Jonny Wilkinson is England's Hero yet again..."

That memorable winning drop kick united the nation, and lead to the start of unprecedented victory celebrations throughout the land. In the split seconds it took for the ball to leave his boot and slip through the posts, Wilkinson's life was to change forever. It wasn't until three days later, when the squad flew back to Heathrow and were met with a rapturous reception, that the enormity of their win, began to sink in.

Like most overnight success stories, Wilkinson's journey has been a long and dedicated one. He spent 16 years 'in rehearsal' before achieving his finest performance, in front of a global audience of 22 million, on that rainy evening in Telstra Stadium, Sydney.

But how did this modest self-effacing 24-year-old become England's new number one son? This biography follows Jonny's journey to international stardom. Find out how he caught the rugby bug, what and who his earliest influences were and what the future holds for our latest English sporting hero.

OTHER BOOKS IN THE SERIES

ROBBIE WILLIAMS

Professionally, things can't get much better for Robbie Williams. In 2002 he signed the largest record deal in UK history when he re-signed with EMI. The following year he performed to over 1.5 million fans on his European tour, breaking all attendance records at Knebworth with three consecutive sell-out gigs.

Since going solo Robbie Williams has achieved five number one hit singles, five number one hit albums; 10 Brits and three Ivor Novello awards. When he left the highly successful boy band Take That in 1995 his future seemed far from rosy. He got off to a shaky start. His nemesis, Gary Barlow, had already recorded two number one singles and the press had virtually written Williams off. But then in December 1997, he released his Christmas single, *Angels.*

Angels re-launched his career – it remained in the Top 10 for 11 weeks. Since then Robbie has gone from strength to strength, both as a singer and a natural showman. His live videos are a testament to his performing talent and his promotional videos are works of art.

This biography tells of Williams' journey to the top – stopping off on the way to take a look at his songs, his videos, his shows, his relationships, his rows, his record deals and his demons.